YouLeadYou™

YouLeadYou™

The Neuroscience of Self-Mastery

NASSER SALEHINIA

A Book of Principles and Practices

Copyright © 2016 by Nasser D. Salehinia

All Right Reserved. No part of this book maybe reproduced or transmitted in any printed or electronic form without the prior written authorization. *The principles, methods, tools and practices described in this book are not intended for healing or therapeutic purposes, and may not be used for any kind of therapeutic, training, coaching or facilitation work without the prior written authorization.*

LIBRARY OF CONGRESS CATALOGING-IN-PUBLICATION DATA
Nasser D. Salehinia

You**LeadYou**: Only you can lead yourself to where you want to go – The Neuroscience of Self-Mastery

Self mastery, self-leadership, neuroscience, and cognition/
Nasser David Salehinia.
1st edition.

Includes bibliographical references
ISBN-13: 978-0692666234
ISBN-10: 0692666230

Cover Design by: Aroosha Sarrafi
Text Design by Mojgan Yusefi

Contact information:
You**LeadYou**
831-200-3460
Info@youleadyou.net
www.youleadyou.net

Advance Praises for YouLeadYou™

The author has taken a unique approach to present the most tangible and practical blend of modern brain and mind sciences I have read. He provides a concise description of how four modes of thinking routinely block our progress, and offers simple scientific tools to overcome them. I highly recommend this book to those who want to transform their lives in practical and enduring ways.

- *Sam Morida, Ph.D.*

This book more than delivers on its premise of demystifying the idea of self-mastery by putting the reader in charge of it. It provides clear understandings and valuable insights based on both modern science and age-old teachings. Its practical exercises and tools allow the readers to take charge of their thoughts, emotions and lives.

- *Peter Harding, M.D.*

I like many things about this book, and in particular I applaud the in-depth scientific research and soul-searching the author has done to be able to explain the concepts clearly while giving the reader a chance to "go it on his/her own" to find the best path to master his/her self.

- *Bradley Winch, Ph.D., J.D.*

Acknowledgments

There are many people I would like to thank including all those that have guided me throughout my years, the authors of every book I have read, as well as the many researchers whose scientific findings and studies have made a major contribution to my work.

In particular, I would like to extend my deepest gratitude to Eugene Khail for all of his valuable input and counsel; to Cricket Raybern, Paul Wagner and Aroosha Sarrafi for their tireless help throughout this project

Thank you all.

Contents

Introduction	1
1. What is Mastery?	3
2. Mastery or Control	9
3. The Premise & The Promise	13
Section 1	22
4. Meet Your Brains	23
5. One Brain -Two Minds	31
6. The Balancing Act	46
7. How Do You Know?	53
8. No Change Allowed	63
9. Why Do You Do That?	67
Section 2	73
10. The Cast of Characters	75
11. The Reacter	84
12. The Ruler	93
13. The Damager	101
14. The Fixer	107
15. Putting it Together	115
16. The Grand Paradox	124
17. Let's be Friends	131
18. Out of My Way Please	145
19. How Can I Really?	166
20. Onward	178

21. Living in Self-Mastery	183
22. Practices Glossary	184

Conclusion

Author's Biography	185
About Us	186
Scientific References	187
General References	193

[Mastery]

Learning who you truly are and developing the skills to lead the life you want

[Self-Mastery]

Intentionally leading yourself toward mastery

Leading yourself toward Self-mastery is neither a philosophical nor esoteric undertaking. Rather, it is a tangible and scientifically describable process at which you can succeed using the right tools

Introduction

Understanding the nature of the mind as a way of getting to better know ourselves and mastering our potentials has been a prominent pursuit of humans since the dawn of civilization. Modern neuroscience has explored the workings of the brain and the mind to help us lead fulfilling lives. Many ancient teachings have taken a holistic approach toward the same goal.

The increasing popularity of neuroscience appears to be another step in that direction. It brings the hope that a scientific approach can finally bring some level of reliability, objectivity, and consistency to the task of understanding the mind, our true natures, and our potentials as human beings.

The challenge is that understanding oneself in a fundamental and profound way cannot be achieved by simply adding more to our knowledge, trying to change our beliefs, following "expert" advice, and wishing to become better and achieve more in our lives.

I have taken a different approach, presenting well-researched aspects of modern neuroscience to clarify teachings about the mind that go back thousands of years. I have used the latest findings in brain and cognitive sciences as a lens to verify age-old teachings and vice versa as a way of bringing objectivity to the task.

Together, they can help us unravel the inner workings of the mind and lead us to right understanding of our essence and potential – offering a simple, practical, and detailed road map for using our minds skillfully to lead more productive and fulfilling lives.

This book also offers simple practices and scientifically-based tools to turn your learnings into practical skills, and lead the life you envision.

I invite you to pause for a few days in your reading after each set of exercises so that you can develop your new skills in daily life.

One

What is Mastery?

The core of mastery lies in the ability to intentionally direct our mind so that, rather than being our master, it works to serve us.

The process of mastery is one of developing skills which then allow us to approach ourselves and life from a different perspective.

Only *we* can lead ourselves toward it; hence the name self-mastery.

Leonardo da Vinci emphasized the significance of self-mastery when he wrote: *"One can have no smaller or greater mastery than mastery of oneself."*

Self-mastery, awakening, self-realization and similar ideas often center on the promise of discovering our true self so that we can live more fulfilling lives.

While typically the domain of organized belief systems and their masters, shamans and gurus, ordinary people have also reached states of mastery, and have tried to share their experiences through advice, books, talks and retreats.

Their intent seems to be that through their teachings, we too can find our way, using their experiences as an example.

Since their experiences do not originate from within us, however, we as listeners, observers and seekers, often find our initial encouragement and inspiration quickly fading away.

The reason is simple: when we follow someone else's experiences, we accumulate *intellectual knowledge*, which is *temporary*. But when we *experience directly*, we integrate our learning deeply and *grow in meaningful and lasting ways*.

In short the journey to self-mastery is quite personal. We *must* experience it for ourselves; only then it becomes useful and lasting.

My own story reflects that very principle. I too was a seeker for many years, read many books, attended retreats, got involved in many practices and traveled the globe in my search for my true self and mastery of my mind. But in the end, the Promised Land remained elusive.

I was always one book, one workshop, or one teacher away. "It" was always waiting for me just around the horizon.

I would become excited about one path or method, and then a trusted friend would recommend another, and that would become my "final answer."

The illusion that I would soon find that master, guru or book encouraged me to become an even more diligent seeker, hoping to finally crack the *secret,* so that I, too, could finally experience real and lasting happiness.

I kept searching for *it,* though, without a clear idea what "it" really was.

Even though this is also a book, it uses a far different approach for recognizing your *own* way by using practical science-based tools for mastering your mind and leading the life you truly want.

As you may have noticed, *I said recognizing, not finding,* because we look to find things that are lost, and recognize what is *already here but unnoticed*. Recognizing our true self, and taking intentional steps to uncover it, is in essence mastering the self.

Does the notion of a true self mean that there also exists a false self? By definition, yes.

The "false" self comes into existence when we use our minds unskillfully, which distorts our thoughts. As the false self becomes more real, distorted thoughts become more prominent in our thinking, and then more convincing. Thus we believe them, act on them and inevitably lead ourselves towards dissatisfied and unproductive lives.

The aim of many ancient teachings has been to show us about the perils of the *false* self, and to offer us an alternative.

Their primary methods center on *motivational advice* such as *let go of the past, let go of judgment, be present, love and trust yourself* and the like. Naturally, we all want that.

But beyond philosophical or theoretical dialogues how can we *really* achieve those?

This is where the brain and cognitive sciences help us gain practical understanding of the way our brains and minds work, how they impact our perceptions and in turn whether we use our minds skillfully enough to step out of the illusion of the false self.

We also know from human history that new knowledge and new tools combined enable us to reach new heights. We rubbed two stones together to create sparks to make fire. We built sharp tools to hunt and feed ourselves.

New tools and new skills, and not simply philosophical understandings, have driven our evolutionary path. They have given us a road map showing us how to master our potentials and evolve ourselves.

As the foundation of this book, therefore, I am using a combination of modern brain and cognitive sciences to validate teachings that date back thousands of years. The intention is to allow readers to directly experience their own unique abilities, and build the skills to release them. This leads to discovery of the true self.

This approach offers four key advantages.

First and most importantly we will explore the notion of self-mastery from several different angles. This brings more objectivity to our process of discovery.

Second, we will take charge of our own discovery by better understanding how our brains and minds function, and how to use them to our advantage.

Third, we will learn how straightforward mastering the self is, once we have the tools and skills needed to achieve it.

And fourth, taking these steps dispels complexity, mystery and authority many believe is necessary to discover who we truly are, and achieve what we genuinely envision in our lives.

The process of self-mastery is, as mentioned earlier, one of the most personal journeys one can imagine.

In short, mastering the self awaken us from the illusions of the false self that come with thinking that we are our thoughts. This allows us to experience who we truly are *beyond* our thoughts, emotions, beliefs, history, judgments, accomplishments, failures, identities or values.

Mastery emerges *only* when we *intentionally lead ourselves* beyond those thoughts and impressions. What follows is an increasing sense of contentment and inner freedom independent of outer circumstances.

It is a deeply calming yet energizing sense which we experience as clarity, confidence, hope, trust, kindness, connectedness and inner strength.

Two things are worth clarifying.

First, self-mastery is a *process* rather than a state or destination. There is no *there* to arrive at, and no "it" to achieve within a given time frame. So there is no discouraging "standard" to live up to. *The journey is the destination itself.*

Second, we already have within us a most powerful ally for succeeding on our journey: *our neurobiology*, as you shall soon see.

As we learn how to use our minds more skillfully, we will become the masters of our lives.

"The greatest discovery of any generation is that human beings can alter their lives by altering the attitude of their minds."
~ Albert Schweitzer

Two

Mastery or Control

Just as important as understanding what mastery is, so is knowing what it is not.

The term mastery is often associated with being fully in "control." And since we are at the center of it, we often interpret this as "self-control" – an idea many religious and philosophical traditions promote as a virtue. In our modern world, self-control indicates strength of character, an achievers' hallmark.

Since the mind creates our idea of the "self," self-control implicitly means "mind-control." Therefore mastering the self means that we must control the mind.

This assumption is false because it proposes to bring the 'out of control' mind under control using the same mind that is already 'out of control.' This does not work.

Why? Because just as the eye cannot see itself, the mind cannot sees itself, and thus its nature and activities are out of its control.

But a more effective alternative beyond "control" is available to us: *mastery*.

==Control and Mastery share a common root: our desire to influence, change or direct conditions in our favor.==

While the differences may be subtle, *control and mastery are vastly different in how we practice them and how they impact our thoughts, emotions, behaviors and results.*

Let's explore the differences:

When we control, we expect reality to be flexible to our wants and desires. But since that expectation is rarely if ever met, desire to control intensifies to grasp at what we want and expect. That is why those who attempt to control constantly up the ante and are never satisfied.

But control in its entirety is nothing but an illusion as it repeatedly fails to accomplish anything useful. It thus simply frustrates and exhausts us, and inevitably becomes coercive.

This coercion damages not only us but also our relationships because even though control may appear to give us a sense of power, it is in reality a *pure expression of powerlessness.*

Acting from a position of powerlessness – control – under any disguise, erodes trust.

While we are at least intellectually aware of the unpleasant side effects of control, it is easy to fall into because our brains, in pursuit of our safety, circulate the illusion that it is necessary to our survival.

That illusion thus drops us into the trap of wanting ever more control, and mind creates lots of noise and fury which convinces us that the trap is real. It therefore becomes hard to escape.

The ultimate trap in control is that it focuses us on noticing, isolating and fixing problems, a trait which becomes habitual over time, and blocks our learning, developing and growing. This reflex is tricky to avoid because this is how our brains and minds have been trained.

Self-Mastery Process

The process of self-mastery avoids that trap by *accepting* reality and *adapting to it*.

Accepting reality, along with focusing on what matters most, pierces through the illusion of control and produces a *humbling effect which is at the heart of true mastery*.

The process of mastery is different in other ways as well.

It is efficient because it exerts its force in measured and sensible ways. Thus it uses less energy to deliver more. This is the reason those who succeed in mastering the self accomplish much while remaining vital and energized.

While self-mastery requires restraint, unlike control it is not coercive. *The more we master the self, the less force and effort we need.*

We need to know what steps are necessary to reach self-mastery. But we first need to accept what takes to accomplish it, and then make a firm decision to follow through irrespective of the distractions that our busy minds and lives constantly present.

At the core of self-mastery is to understand how the mind works, and to skillfully direct it. Leading the self toward mastery starts an upward spiral, a process which becomes increasingly easier with time and practice.

A master musician never coerces the instrument, yet produces pleasing sounds. A master singer doesn't strain her voice, as it will destroy her performance and career, yet she reaches extraordinary notes and pitches.

The same applies in this personal journey: self-mastery offers us a high level of proficiency in handling complex and demanding conditions of life – allowing us to respond skillfully and live life fully.

"You will never have a greater or lesser dominion than that over yourself...the height of a man's success is gauged by his self-mastery; the depth of his failure by his self-abandonment."

~ Leonardo da Vinci

Three

The Premise and the Promise

I would like to share with you both the premise and the promise of this book so we have a framework as we move forward.

The premise of this book is based on two principles.

The first principle began with a personal story. While traveling through Asia in early 2006, I decided to change my plans and join a ten day silent meditation program at a modest monastery on the outskirts of Chiang Mai in Northern Thailand. As a foreigner I was given a room about 8x20 feet, furnished with foam on top of a small wooden platform for a bed, a pillow and blanket, and a small light.

The retreat started with an orientation informing us of the practice schedule: 45 minutes of sitting meditation followed by 45 minutes of walking meditation. We were to start with six hours of practice per day and gradually increase it over the next 10 days to 20 hours per day. The only meals were served at 5:30 and 10 a.m. and consisted of some kind of broth with small pieces of tofu or beans, if someone had made a donation that day. We were also to meet with the meditation teacher at 3 p.m. daily to ask questions and receive instruction for the next day's practice.

I started confidently since this was not my first silent retreat. I had done others of up to 30 days without much challenge. But this one was turning out differently. My mind became so obsessed with stories about the tasteless food, the uncomfortable bed and so on, that not only did the quality of my practice quickly became dreadful, I also missed my meetings with the meditation teacher for the first two days! If not for the knock on my door from the coordinator concerned about my well-being and whereabouts, I would have perhaps missed other appointments as well.

I quickly made my way to the other building and soon I was sitting in front of this small-framed teacher who in his gentle way asked how I was doing. While telling him about aches in my body due to continuous sitting and walking practice, and the lack of a comfortable bed, and the rest of my complaints, he gently asked me, "Would you like to cry a bit?" Only then did I realize that tears were running down my cheeks. I quickly wiped my face, and after a few more minutes of talking with him, I returned to my little room to continue with my practice.

To my surprise, "something" had shifted within me which I started noticing as I sat down to practice. My mind was clearer and focused throughout the day. I slept like a baby that night. I woke up refreshed when the breakfast bell rang at 5 a.m. And the food ... to my greatest surprise, it tasted just fine, even good! Where did all of that come from, I started wondering.

In my next meeting, the teacher asked if my body was still hurting. When I shared with him all that had transpired since our talk the day before, he softly asked me, "What happened?"

"I don't know," I responded. He repeated that question a few times and received the same answer from me: "I don't know." I, too, became curious after that exchange!

He then asked me this question: *"Could it be that your mind creates all of your suffering?"* "I believe so," I replied. I had just experienced freedom from the agony my thoughts and stories had spun over the past few days.

He then proceeded to tell me the following story which became the foundation of my thoughts that led me to write this book.

Siddhartha Gautama, the prince who left his opulent life to experience what he had witnessed as "ordinary" life on his rare outings from the palace, first became a hermit to make up for his lavish life style. Realizing that the answer does not exist in extremes, he sought out the wisdom of masters and philosophers throughout northern India over the next five years. *"No one knows,"* Siddhartha uttered afterwards. He then vowed to sit in meditation until he awakened from that which he considered to be the illusions of the mind, and the root of all human suffering. After six months of sitting in meditation under the Bodhi tree, he declared that he had awakened from the illusions of the mind, and thus he became the Buddha, the awakened one.

In response to questions about how he found awakening and what he looked for, the Buddha responded: *"I did not look for anything.* All I did was to *rightly understand the inner working of my mind* and realized that *its foundation is based on fear.* Once I shined the *light of awareness on my fears, they vanished and awakening, always existing, showed up on its own."*

"Are you telling me not to look for "awakening" and instead to remove the obstacles that my mind invents – such as fear – that prevent me from experiencing my true self?" I asked the teacher. *"You understand rightly,"* he replied.

I left the retreat energized and with a new perspective about the path to my true self, which I had started 28 years earlier. As I contemplated my conversations with the teacher over the days and weeks that followed, *"understanding the inner working of the mind"* kept circulating in my mind.

What does that mean, really? This question kept popping in my mind.

Right understanding, according to teachings of Buddha, occurs when we use our minds skillfully. This then leads us to recognize things *as they really are*.

In practical terms, skillful use of our minds involves: directly experiencing something rather than relying on the opinions of others, not having preconceived ideas, not jumping to conclusions, considering explanations and views that are different from our own, taking our time in drawing conclusions, being open to changing our opinion when presented with facts that contradict it, and finally, not mistaking a part for the whole.

That teaching, as I understood it at the time, however, did not quite satisfy my curiosity about the *inner working of the mind* which I had been told about.

In my continued pursuit, I came across what the Dalai Lama

repeatedly says, that Buddhism is a philosophy centered on mind training, and that if any of its claims do not stand up to the *scrutiny of science*, they should be changed or discarded.

This opened a new door and encouraged me to take a scientific approach to investigating the *inner working of the mind*.

Luckily, I had been fortunate enough to gain some background about the brain and mind, in prior years, through apprenticeship with two experts in the field.

My first mentor was Dr. Stan Grof, the renowned psychiatrist and brain researcher. My second was another brilliant psychiatrist Dr. Peter Harding. Their work, along with my own research, teaching and practice, provided me the foundation.

In the course of my inquiry, I came across other teachers who also recommended removing the inner obstacles as the way to recognizing our true self. For instance, Rumi, the 13th century Persian poet, mystic and scholar says: *"Your task is not to seek for love, but merely to seek and find all the barriers within yourself that you have built against it."*

I spent the next nine years, starting in 2007, researching and exploring the brain and mind phenomenon from many angles, both scientifically, theoretically and philosophically.

This exhaustive outward search, and inward practice led me to realize that *removing the mind's limiting forces that act as barriers through the right understanding of what they exactly are, and how they function offers a far simpler and more practical route than looking for the illusive self.*

Therefore, what exactly those mind barriers are, how they function to create a restraining force that continually block our progress, and most importantly how to free our self from them became the first principle of this book.

The second principle of this book is simplicity. Albert Einstein expresses it beautifully: "*If you cannot explain it simply, you don't understand it well enough.*"

Why simplicity? Because human nature and common sense allow us to comprehend and retain information better when it is explained in a tangible and practical way.

These two principles form the premise of this book. I will offer my findings as to how the brain and mind instinctively block our progress and cause unhappiness, and offer simple tools to overcome those restraining forces.

I will also do my very best to share all of that as simply and briefly as I know how.

As the author I have objectively investigated that which I am sharing here, have put it into practice, and have tried to write using my own experiences as much as possible.

The promise of this book is *you*, because *only* you and no one else can lead you to your true self and your innate potentials.

Even though everything you need to know for your self-discovery is already within you, it is essential to *directly* and *inwardly experience* your learning in ways that allow you to use your mind skillfully in *all* areas of your life.

As always we have options. You can read through this book, add it to your knowledge, and move on to the next book, seminar or teacher. You can also decide to *understand* it, practice the tools offered, build new skills and lead the life you truly want.

Knowledge and Understanding

Why is it important to distinguish between knowledge and understanding when working in the realm of the mind?

Because the mind processes all information as soon as it receives it, we gain knowledge fairly quickly, for instance by reading a book, hearing a lecture or watching a movie.

Let's consider an example. We study a foreign language for number of years, learn certain words, and even master its linguistic structure. However, when we try to speak it, we find that knowledge alone is different than the skill to speak it fluently. That ability comes only with time and practice.

It takes longer for the brain to develop understanding and turn it in into experience than it does to just accumulate knowledge. It is only when we put knowledge into practice that we gain understanding, develop experiences and in turn literally rewire and reshape our brain.

How Do We Come to know?

We come to know by identifying, naming, categorizing and recalling information. We identify a tree as a maple; we name colors in the rainbow; we categorize people by their behavior, and we recall phone numbers.

Knowing, however, is temporary. If we don't use a phone number for a while, we tend to forget it, and have to look it up again.

Let's examine how the same process, gaining only temporary knowledge, applies to personal development.

In our pursuit of our true self, we listen to a lecture by a person known to have gone far in his or her journey *of* self-mastery.

This excites us, and we thus ask ourselves *why reinvent the wheel* when we can more easily achieve the same results by following their path?

So we participate in their teachings and leave with great excitement, thinking that we too have finally found the "answers." That motivate us to envision life-changing decisions which at the time we are convinced without doubt we will accomplish.

And then, as life would have it, we face unexpected challenges to which the solution was not offered as part of the knowledge passed on to us. We then become perplexed as to how to handle those challenges. We become demotivated. Our search for "other" and "better" answers resumes.

Now let's explore how understanding – combining knowledge with practice to develop skill – is a more effective path.

When we understand, we are able to distinguish, explain, interpret, and make sense of information directly by ourselves. This allows us to learn and develop personal experiences with which we can adapt to handle life's natural and unforeseen ups and downs more effectively.

This is right understanding: using our minds to identify reality, adapt to it, and to skillfully address our unique challenges by deciding in real time what is best for us. This real-time awareness allows us to *recognize the entanglements* of our thoughts, *sidestep them*, and lead our minds effectively.

Thus when we consciously put knowledge into practice and develop personal experience, skill and mastery will follow.

Right understanding thus allows us to skillfully direct our thoughts, and make changes at the mind and brain levels that are real and lasting.

"The highest activity a human being can attain is learning for understanding, because to understand is to be free" is how the Dutch philosopher Baruch Spinoza views the importance of right understanding.

So, it's really up to you.

"We do not become enlightened - we discover our enlightenment, which has always been there."

~ Sakyong Mipham

Section 1

In section 1 we will explore how our brains and minds work to create our life experiences.

In this process we will gain a practical understanding as to how the working of our brains and minds influence our thoughts, and in turn our emotions, behaviors and ultimately the quality of our lives.

We will learn, by exploring key elements of modern brain and cognitive sciences, how thoughts either lead us closer to mastering the self and living the life we envision, or further away from it.

We'll then learn specific neuroscience-based methods and tools that allow us to free ourselves from thoughts and emotions that act as a restraining force blocking our path to our self.

Going forward, I will refer to our true self simply as the Self.

Doing the short exercises at the end of selected chapters is key to building your skills. Consider making a habit of using the tools throughout your day. With practice, you will become more skilled at directing your mind, and in turn become productive and in charge of every aspect of your life.

Practice makes perfect.

Four

Meet Your Brains

The brain is the body's control center and manages every aspect of our biological and emotional lives, including our heart rate, blood pressure, digestion, immune system and sexual drive, as well as our feelings, learning, dreaming and memory.

The brain masterfully and seamlessly performs all the functions that make us human.

It fashions our thoughts, hopes, dreams, and imaginations, and has enabled humans to achieve breathtaking milestones in science, medicine, art, music and literature.

The process of evolution, which ranks *survival as primary*, followed by our desires to thrive and connect, has given us three unique brain sections: the reptilian, the limbic, and the neocortex. While independent, they are deeply connected and naturally influence one another.

Understanding how the brain receives information, and the complex ways in which it processes it, will be helpful as we start learning how to more effectively shape our brains.

Here are the three section of the brain:

The old (reptilian) brain is the oldest of the three and in charge of controlling the body's basic vital functions. Since our survival depends on the proper working of the body, this part of the brain *always operates* in "'survival mode." It therefore responds instantly, without much discernment, to protect us from potential harm, and remains fixed and not open to change.

The Feeling (limbic) brain deals with emotions such as anger, happiness and fear, as well as memories. It generates our emotions that lead us to developing values, which in turn influence our thoughts and behaviors.

The New brain (neocortex) is involved in higher-order thinking, such as logic, problem solving, decision making and imagination. It is flexible, open to change, and holds nearly infinite learning abilities.

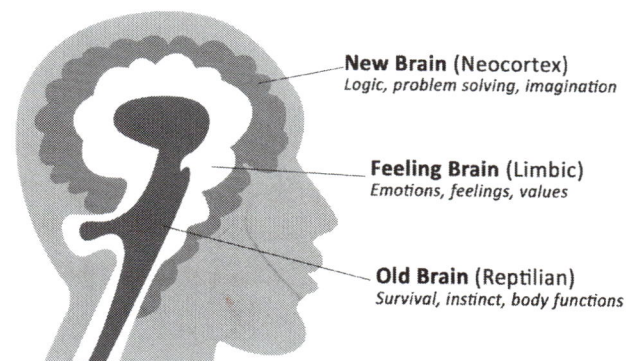

New Brain (Neocortex)
Logic, problem solving, imagination

Feeling Brain (Limbic)
Emotions, feelings, values

Old Brain (Reptilian)
Survival, instinct, body functions

Together, these three sections of the brain engage in two-way communication with the body through a vast web of nerves in the spinal cord. Jointly these are known as the central nervous system and the brain acts as its conductor.

The entire brain is about three pounds of spongy tissue consisting of about 100 billion specialized cells called neurons.

Each neuron connects to up to 10,000 others, passing signals via as many as 1,000 trillion synaptic connections. These synapses pass information at the rate of 1-100 times per second throughout the brain. Thus, *information crosses the brain in a tenth of a second.* [1]

In computer terms, the brain processes around 1 trillion bits of data per second. That is a great deal of information moving very quickly through about three pounds of spongy tissue. In addition, the brain creates 1 followed by a million zeros possible states – temporary conditions such as thoughts or emotions – at any moment. [2,3,4]

The brain needs a great amount of energy to do all that work. It therefore consumes 20-25 percent of our oxygen intake, blood flow and glucose. [5,6]

The brain is known as the most complex and fastest structure so far discovered. It is complex enough that scientists, even with the most sophisticated modern tools at our disposal, have identified only about 10 percent of what it actually does. The other 90 percent remains a mystery. [7,8]

Your Brain at Work

Let's explore how we experience the working of the brain and how it shapes our thoughts, emotions and behaviors.

The brain functions on many levels, including:

1. It remains alert all the time, though at varying rates during rest or activity, to do its primary job of keeping us safe.

2. The brain evolved as a tool to protect us from potential harm, anticipate and overcome danger, and solve our survival related problems. Like radar, it constantly scans our inner and outer worlds for potential threats, and fights anything that it perceives as such to our safety, whether internally or externally.

This is how: A double almond-shaped mass of cells called the amygdala, located deep within the reptilian part of the brain, processes incoming signals and turns them into emotions soon after they enter the brain. The amygdala enables us to feel emotions and to perceive them in others. It senses the nature of our thoughts about ourselves, others and events, and how they make us feel.

The amygdala uses 2/3 of its capacity five times per second to continually search, mostly through our sight and hearing, to find *what is and may not be right.* In essence, it looks for negative, threatening stimuli, within us and in our environments, to alert us in time so we can keep ourselves safe.

The large volume of negative information the amygdala constantly collects and processes, plus its built in threat-detecting ability, *makes the brain a magnet for negativity. This negativity bias deeply influences our thoughts, emotions, behaviors, learning and motivation.* [9]

3. The brain also *perceives any attempts to change or improve as a potential threat to our survival* and quickly builds defenses against it.

4. The amygdala quickly sends the negative emotions it collects to long-term subconscious memory. The memory system then stores and organizes negative information in such a way that they are more vivid and faster to recall than positive ones.

   The brain takes this counter-intuitive approach so as to have immediate access to all threatening information. It considers what we label as "negative" to be survival knowledge it might need to protect us. [10]

5. The brain stores positive information in short-term memory since it poses no threat to us. The brain sends this information to long-term memory only if *we intentionally focus on it for 10-20 seconds at the time it happens; otherwise it will soon fade from memory. This makes the brain like Teflon that repels positive information.*

6. The brain is concerned neither with objectivity nor reality, nor does it understand values such as good, bad, right, wrong, positive, negative, sad or happy. It has a single focus: protecting our survival.

7. The brain accepts all incoming information as true, whether true or not. Let's do an experiment: Imagine you have just cut a fresh lime in half and are squeezing the juice in your mouth. Taste its sourness.

For most people, saliva will start flowing even though you've *imagined* all of this.

8. The brain has no concept of time. *Everything happens right here and right now.*

   Let's do another experiment: Think for a second about a past incident that upset you. Remember your emotions about it. Stop reading and notice your body sensations.

   Most people report increased heart rate and sense of agitation as if the incident were happening right now. *As far as your brain is concerned, it is.*

   Try the same experiment with another past event about a pleasant and enjoyable experience. Stop reading and notice your body sensations. A sense of relaxation is what most people experience.

   Time and accuracy are meaningless to the brain as it cannot afford to lose precious time to interpret meaning and timing, since its primary mission is to protect us.

9. We use our entire brain all the time since it is an extremely connected network of circular loops. The myth that we only use 10 percent of our brains, and that Einstein's atypical intelligence is attributed to him using a few percentage points more, is just that, a myth. In fact, autopsy results have shown that Einstein's brain was smaller than average. [11,12,13]

10. Since the entire brain is deeply interconnected, it functions through association – any thought or memory triggers similar ones. When we are hungry our minds

flood with thoughts about food – what kind, where, and how soon – rather than thoughts about showering or car repair. Similarly, **when we entertain fear-based thoughts, other anxiety producing thoughts flood our minds.**

One More Brain

Surprisingly enough, in addition to the brains located in our heads, we have one more, called the heart-brain, located under the ribs in our chests.

Research by neurologist Dr. Andrew Amour and the Institute of HeartMath has revealed that the heart has a complex nervous system of around 40,000 neurons. It contains neurotransmitters, proteins and support cells similar to those found in the head-brain. Its elaborate circuitry enables it to learn, remember, and even feel and sense. It is named the "Little Brain," and it acts independently of the head-brain. [14,15]

The heart generates a continuous series of powerful electromagnetic pulses to communicate information to the head-brain and the body. Its electromagnetic field is about 5,000 times stronger than the brain's and can be detected from several feet away from the body. [16,17]

The heart-brain sends information such as feeling sensations to the head-brain through several nerve pathways. When the heart functions in a stable and coherent way, we experience the information it send to the head-brain as heightened mental clarity, improved perception, performance, decision making, and creativity. This allows us to experience the state of feeling alive and energetic. [18,19,20]

When we experience emotions such as love, compassion, creativity and gratitude, the heart becomes more coherent, and sends that information to the head-brain and the entire body. This happens neurologically, biophysically and biochemically, establishing a positive feedback loop between the heart, brain and body, which benefits us in major ways. [21,22,23]

Research also indicates that when people are in close proximity or touch each other, their brains and heart waves synchronize with each other. Even when two people are at a conversational distance, the electromagnetic signals generated by one person's heart can influence the other person's brain rhythms. [24,25,26]

As we can see, we humans are deeply interconnected within ourselves as well as with other living beings.

In the next chapter, we will explore our amazing central nervous system even further, and examine how functioning of the brain fashions what we call *the mind*.

Five

One Brain - Two Minds

We often use the words brain and mind interchangeably. But even though they overlap, they are two distinct systems.

The brain is the physical and visible organ, consisting of billions of neurons and connections, whose dynamic working creates impulses we call thoughts, which then form the building blocks of what we call the mind.

The mind is our invisible thinking machine. It constantly gathers perceptions from our inner and outer worlds with which it produces our thoughts that lead to our emotions, memory, imagination, reason, understanding and finally, behavior.

In short, *the mind* expresses the working of *the brain*.

We use our brains to transmit electrochemical signals that automatically manage hundreds of bodily functions behind the scenes to coordinate our motions and activities.

We use our minds to think and ponder about such things as self, others and events. Thoughts express the working of the mind.

The human mind's ability to analyze, understand and solve complex problems by using differing modes of thinking – logic, reason, evaluation, association, comparison and contrast – is what sets us apart from nearly all other living beings.

Using the mind skillfully we have found causes of disease such as viruses, bacteria, genetic defects, environmental factors, lifestyle and stress. We have developed intricate devices to detect everything from the invisible ultraviolet range to the properties of a single atom.

As we see, we can use the mind as a tool to gain knowledge, wisdom and balance.

We can also use it to create chaos, suffering, stagnation, individual and societal malaise and decline.

We can trace both effects throughout human history.

Now that we have definitions of the brain and the mind, why does the title above talks about *two* minds?

Because the brain has a cognitive network consisting of two parts, each doing something different. Let's first have a clear definition of what cognition is and does.

We use cognition to make sense of the information the brain produces such as when we think, learn, understand, remember, judge and solve problems. Both of the brain's networks facilitate these activities.

Let's experience these two parts directly through a practice.

Recall a memory that causes you distress or unhappiness. Let thoughts about it fill your mind. Allow this to go on for around 5-10 seconds. Put the book aside and do this now. Notice how you feel in your mind and body.

Next, put your thumb and index and middle fingers together and begin rubbing them against each other. Imagine you are trying to determine the quality of a fabric through your sense of touch.

When your attention wanders, gently bring it back to the sensation between your fingers. Pay close attention to how the rubbing of your fingers against each other feel until you become fully absorbed in it. Every time your mind wonders, bring it back to the sensation of your fingers rubbing against each other. Put the book aside and do this for around 10 seconds. Notice how you feel.

Next, continue the rubbing action while trying to think about the distressing thoughts you had before. If you notice them surfacing, pay even closer attention to the sensation that rubbing your fingers against each other is producing. Put the book aside and do this for another 10 seconds. Notice your thoughts and how you feel in your body.

If your experience is similar to people I have in my workshops, the distressing thoughts start losing their grip, and give way to a state of relative calm and spaciousness.

What's happened? You've created mental calm by engaging a part of your cognitive network through using your sense of touch. *This automatically switched off the other part of the network which stores distressing thoughts and memories.*

Let's explore the scientific aspects of both brain networks in more detail, starting with the one that activates distressing experiences.

The Cognitive Network

Nearly three decades of neuroscience research and brain imaging have verified the existence of a *Default Mode Network,* or DMN in the brain. [27,28,29,30,31] It is called default mode because it is our *habitual go-to place* when we are awake and focused internally rather than on external tasks.

The DMN is a large collection of integrated neural webs like a complex electrical circuit. Through the DMN we daydream, remember, imagine, evaluate and judge. [32,33]

How does the mind behave when in default mode? It becomes past and future oriented and wonders about what has happened and what may happen, primarily focused on the self.

In short, the mind in *default mode* becomes *past and future oriented.* This unconscious involvement unsettles the mind since it has no predictable control over the past or the future, which the brain considers critical to our safety. It therefore *perceives itself as losing control*, which leads it to becoming alarmed about our safety. This panicking agitates and unsettles the mind.

The agitated mind becomes ruminative, repeating the same negative thoughts and stories again and again. This retelling soon becomes obsessive, and since the brain is already alarmed, it in turn centers our attention on our personal safety. So the mind's repetitive negative thoughts and stories increasingly center on self. In other words, *we become self-centered*.

Once self-centered -- with personal safety concerns operating in the background -- we involuntarily become anxious and then reactive. We unconsciously become rigid, insecure and mistrusting, and in turn our minds become even more anxious and fearful, and continue to contract.

In that state we give undue credibility to, and become negatively impacted by, *what we think of ourselves* and how we think *others view* us.

But those thoughts are *only guesswork,* artifacts *the anxious mind* creates based on *little or no fact or reality*. As this process continues, the mind grows even more fearful.

The brain interprets this increasing fear as a *true* and *definite* sign of danger since it cannot differentiate fact from fiction, the mind becomes even more rigid and the harmful cycles continues.

Multiple studies have demonstrated that this cycle is the most common cause of mental unrest, which leads to other harmful conditions including chronic stress, depression, hypertension, inability to focus, lack of motivation, negative moods and mood swings, insomnia, addiction and illnesses. [34,35,36,37,38,39,40]

The Neuroscience of the DMN

How do these fearful mental states form in the first place?

As you recall, the amygdala, our brain's danger detector, continually looks for *what's not right* in our inner and outer worlds. It will ultimately find something and alerts the brain, which becomes alarmed and then reactive.

The brain's reactivity leads the amygdala to look for and produce even more "threatening" information.

Also, the amygdala constantly interacts with long-term memory where past negative experiences and beliefs are stored. Influenced by them, the brain grows even more agitated and reactive, which we experience as increasing tension in the mind and body.

From a scientific perspective, *when neurons fire, the brain's interconnected loops stimulate others to fire similarly. Neurons that fire together wire together – and vice versa. When fear-neurons fire, the brain's fear-based circuitry becomes stronger and more dominant.*

As a result our thoughts, emotions and behaviors become increasingly ineffectual, and we become limited in our ability to productively use our minds.

Because of these limitations, I refer to the default mode network (DMN) as the small mind since it defines and confines us in many ways. The small mind is anxious, self-centered, reactive, inefficient, insecure, mistrusting, inflexible and chaotic. I lives in the past and future.

Here is how the small mind activates and negatively impacts us:

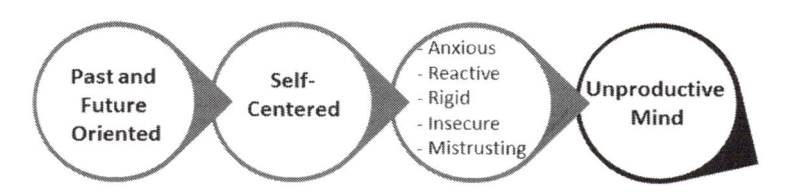

Past and Future Oriented → Self-Centered → Anxious, Reactive, Rigid, Insecure, Mistrusting → Unproductive Mind

Two key points about the small mind:

It easily absorbs our attention without our awareness since it is our *default mode with which we are familiar and comfortable*. For example, most of us have missed an exit on a freeway while absorbed in our thoughts until we realize we are lost.

We must therefore remain watchful of the small mind's runaway habits.

The small mind plays on our vulnerabilities, again without our awareness, by convincing us we are in harm's way and that is protecting us, even when *actual* danger does *not* exist.

The small mind, using a combination of those factors sneaks up on us from behind, and distorts our thoughts.

The Other Network

Now that we understand the small mind, let's look at the other part of our cognitive network: the *Task-positive Network* (TPN).

This network engages when we use one or more of our five physical senses, especially primary ones such as seeing, hearing and touching. Some examples: when we listen to sounds, watch the sunset or ocean waves, hug a loved one or feel the sensation of warm water on our skin when taking a shower.

The Task Positive Network (TPN) also engages when we focus our minds on external tasks such as gardening, watching a movie, working out, whistling or drawing. In doing these type of activities we focus our senses externally, and *automatically activate the TPN*. [41,42,43]

Basically, we activate the TPN when we *intentionally engage one* or more of our physical senses in the *present moment*. In doing so, we gain in significant ways.

Let's explore:

The DMN is past- and future-oriented, which sets off the small mind and its ill effects. Therefore, when we get caught in the small mind (DMN), *we habitually battle thoughts with more thoughts, which produces even more distress and distortions in our minds.*

On the other hand, the TPN operates only in the *here and now*, where anxiety, insecurity, mistrust and fear cannot survive. This process begins the moment we interrupt the small mind's obsessive negative thoughts and stories by engaging the TPN using one of our physical senses through a physical or mental activity. *This automatically disengages the small mind.* This is what you did with the finger rubbing exercise.

Why does this happen? Because, scientifically speaking, *we only have enough mental power to run a single network at a time.* We simply cannot be in the past, future and present at the same time.

We have enough mental power to operate only one network at a time.

Therefore, by engaging the TPN through our senses, we can simply bypass the small mind's *limiting forces* altogether.

"The secret of change" as Socrates said *"is to focus all of your energy, not on fighting the old, but on building the new."*

These three facts are of utmost importance:

1. *We have the mental power to run only one network at a time.* When The TPN is on, the small mind (DMN) automatically turns off, and vice versa. [44,45,46,47]

   The relationship between the two networks is similar to inhaling and exhaling. Despite their essential connection, they cannot occur at the same time. They operate like a seesaw which, as we shall see, is a gift of our neurobiology.

   This diagrams shows the two network's seesaw effect, and that *all* we need to do to benefit from TPN is to quiet the DMN. (small mind)

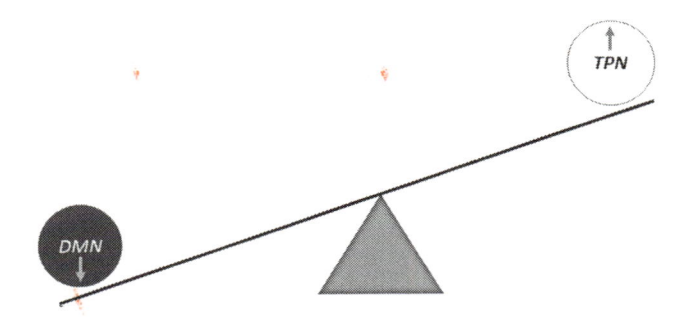

   Remember that we have erratic attention spans that shifts easily. We use one of our senses to engage the TPN and gain release from the small mind only to be interrupted in the next second by a rush of thoughts as it takes over and the TPN turns off.

SENSES!!

The key is to practice using our senses to repeatedly activate the TPN. This builds and strengthens the neural pathways and connections in the brain that allow us to do so more easily.

2. The small mind (DMN) and TPN, despite their opposing natures, must work in balance for us to function properly in our daily lives. When they do, we are able to use their abilities to our benefit. For example, when TPN is engaged, we can *objectively* consider past events to improve our present and future actions. We more clearly remember important details, avoid repeating past errors, and effectively plan and organize our daily tasks.

3. As we learn to engage the TPN more often, it becomes a bridge into our higher cognitive capabilities, which are scientifically known as *Executive Functions*. [48,49]

Thus the TPN functions *as a bridging network* – allowing us to move ourselves from the small mind to our higher-order cognitive abilities.

What are Executive Functions?

Executive Functions are a series of *higher-order* cognitive abilities that the new brain (neocortex) makes possible. They allow us to consciously steer our perception, thought, emotion and behavior toward achieving our goals in balanced ways. [50,51]

How? The neocortex, where these functions originate, allows us to establish and maintain the crucial balance between the DMN (small mind) and the TPN (bridge network).

use this for EI

This ability, scientifically known as *emotional regulation*, allows us to bring the impulsive small mind under our direction, and use our higher-order cognitive abilities to monitor, organize and lead ourselves to achieve our objectives. [52,53,54,55,56,57]

How can Executive Functions accomplish all that? When we engage the present-oriented TPN, we too become present in how we think, feel and behave in *real-time*. The mind thus comes out of its past and future obsessing and settles into its calm natural state.

The calm mind is inherently perceptive, responsive, organized and resilient. It is the door to our higher-order cognitive abilities, allowing us to dynamically make necessary changes to our thinking, emotions and behaviors to reach our goals. [58,59,60]

When we tap into our Executive Functions, we thus open up to adapting, relearning, developing and growing. **We thus become increasingly productive.**

I refer to the part of the mind that opens up by the executive functions as the BIG mind. The big mind is productive, confident, responsive, resilient, organized and intuitive. It operates in the present moment.

We all possess the BIG mind. It's built-in. All we need to do is to intentionally use it more often which will develop and grow it further.

Here is how the big mind engages and benefits us:

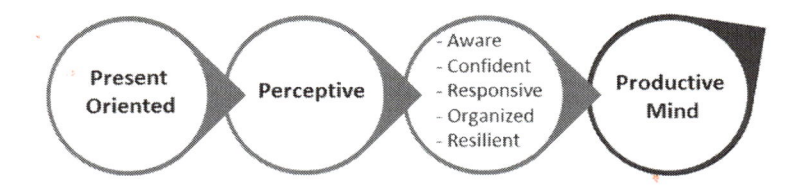

```
Present Oriented → Perceptive → - Aware / - Confident / - Responsive / - Organized / - Resilient → Productive Mind
```

As we can see, living a productive, creative and satisfied life does not require fighting day in and day out – our inherent neurobiology offers us an easier and more effective way. Leading the self -- Self-leadership -- is the main tool we need to get there. Mastering that skill is what this books offers.

Self-mastery is the skill of intentionally leading the mind toward its calm natural state, which automatically makes it productive.

We have been able to achieve amazing feats over the course of our evolution when we use our minds productively.

The harnessing of fire, the discovery of penicillin, and the decoding of the human genome are some remarkable examples of what transpires when the mind wanders – as it does during a walk on the beach or listening to music. It is during these periods that answers to "unresolvable" problems emerge without us consciously searching for them.

How does this happen? With the small mind's ability to daydream, we contemplate challenges, and by using the bridge network, we can tap into our big mind for answers.

Our big mind can be compared to the conductor of a symphony orchestra, skillfully coordinating players and their instruments to achieve pleasing results. ***This is similar to***

when our thoughts, emotions and behaviors are playing in harmony.

There's a story of a wise old Cherokee teaching his grandson about life. *"There is a fight that is always going on inside me,"* he explains to the boy. *"It is a terrible fight and it is between two wolves. One wolf is negative - he has anger, envy, sorrow, regret, greed, arrogance, self-pity, guilt, resentment, inferiority, lies, false pride, superiority, and ego."* However, he continued, *"The other wolf is good - he is joy, peace, love, hope, serenity, humility, kindness, benevolence, empathy, generosity, truth, compassion, and faith. The same fight is going on inside you - and inside every other person, too."* The grandson thinks about it for a minute and then asks his grandfather, *"Which wolf inside me will win?"* The old Cherokee simply replies, *"The one you feed."*

The key is choosing which of our minds to feed.

As Buckminster Fuller put it: *"You never change things by fighting the existing reality. To change something, build a new model that makes the existing model obsolete."*

In other words, feed the mind that helps you reach the life model you envision: the *big mind*.

Practice

The next time you feel anxious and experience agitation, remind yourself that:

- The small mind is active behind the scenes. Believing its stories does not serve you in any way.

- Remember that you only have the mental power to maintain one network at a time.

- **_Make a conscious choice_** and use the finger rubbing exercise you did earlier to quickly move yourself to the big mind. Continue until you notice a release in your mind and body from anxiety and tension.

Key Points Summary

We have covered a great deal of scientific information in this section. Let's summarize the important points:

In our brains we have two information processing networks; the default mode network (DMN/small mind), and the task positive network (TPN/bridge).

The small mind, centered on the DMN, is past and future-oriented, self-centered, reactive, and fearful. It easily becomes obsessive, protective and resistant to learning and growing.

The other network, the TPN/bridge, is present-oriented and allows us to move ourselves from the small mind to our big mind by intentionally engaging our senses.

Within our big mind emotions such as anxiety, self-centeredness, insecurity, judgment, worry cannot survive for long. We therefore become more objective, expansive, and progressive in our thinking, feeling and behavior, and able to achieve our goals in productive ways.

Remember: *you need not overpower the small mind. All you need to do is to move yourself to the big mind, and distressing thoughts will automatically dissolve.*

Rumi, the 13th-century Persian poet, scholar and mystic, used the term *small mind* to point to the mind's self-centered, reactive modes which innately *define* and *confine* us. He used the term *big mind* to point to the open, ever-present and dynamic mind which naturally *harmonizes* and *expands* us.

Other ancient and contemporary teachers including Jesus, Buddha, Lao Tzu, Gandhi, Martin Luther King, Jr., Dogen, Nelson Mandela, D.T. Suzuki, Mother Theresa and St. Francis of Assisi, among others, have all described the confining effects of the small mind, and the open dynamic nature of the big mind, in their own unique expressions.

Going forward, we'll be looking at how the small mind and big mind relate to mastering the Self.

"It's hard to give unlimited power to a limited mind."

~ Nicholas Tesla

Six

The Balancing Act

In the previous chapter we learned the crucial role that balance plays in every aspect of our lives. Let's look at what the brain, the director of our existence, does to achieve this balance.

Maintaining *continual balance is key to our survival* because our physical and emotional systems rely on a stable environment to function properly and sustain our well-being.

To achieve this the brain uses our five senses to constantly monitor our internal and external environments to maintain a relative state balance known as homeostasis. [61,62,63]

Much of the brain's elaborate balancing activity takes place beyond our awareness. But whenever our internal thermostat becomes imbalanced, we experience emotional stress, and then our body follows.

This imbalance starts a *negative feedback loop* which signals our neurobiological system to step in, adjust and restore our physical and emotional balance as quickly as possible. For example, when our body needs energy, we get the urge to eat, when exhausted we want to rest, and when lonely we want to connect with others.

We generate imbalance whenever we conclude, *accurately* or *not*, that we are unable to satisfactorily deal with whatever is occurring at the moment. We experience this imbalance as stress because we become concerned that we may be physically or emotionally vulnerable.

We become stressed whenever we believe, accurately or not, that we cannot successfully deal with what is occurring within or outside of ourselves.

The brain interprets this feeling of vulnerability as a threat to our safety, and the *mind creates the sensation of fear* to motivate us to act and overcome this perceived "threat" as quickly as possible.

The brain then signals the region that controls our stress-response system – known as the hypothalamus – to release specific hormones.

Once released, our sense of balance starts restoring and the previously opened negative feedback loop closes.

This balancing process works the same way our home thermostat does. We feel cold and increase the temperature to 76 degrees. The thermostat signals a central unit to kick in and remain on until that temperature has been reached.

From then on, when the thermostat registers any change from 76 degrees, it opens a negative feedback loop responding to that change. This initiates specific action to restore balance, and closes the loop once finished.

Similarly, when we are under stress, the brain opens a negative feedback loop which signals our stress-response system to release hormones until it restores balance. Once finished, our thermostat sends positive feedback signal to our brain that its job is complete, and it goes on standby until its intervention once again becomes necessary.

If a negative loop remains open, the central heating and cooling unit will continue running until it causes actual damage to itself and eventually the structure.

In the same manner, we will cause physical and emotional damage to ourselves when constant stress becomes a way of life and we remain in a reactive state.

How We Become Reactive

How do imbalance and reactivity form in the brain in the first place?

The neocortex, where rational thinking takes place, shares major connections with the amygdala, the region which constantly looks for *what's not right* and produces the impulses of anxiety and fear.

Under normal conditions the neocortex releases specific neurochemicals to regulate the amygdala and slow it down, decreasing our reactive stress-response. We therefore *respond* in suitable ways to whatever situation we are facing. For example, if we are waiting in a busy checkout line and become anxious, the proper response – if the purchase is in our long-term best interest – is to tolerate the frustration, and wait to complete our purchase.

However, *when we are under stress, our neurobiological process described above reverses itself.*

Let's see how:

The amygdala under constant stress increases in volume, growing its capacity to collect more negative information. It then directs the brain's hypothalamus to deliver specific hormones to the neocortex, effectively shutting down our access to our rational thinking. We therefore become more stressed and reactive. This lead to the amygdala increasing in volume and collecting even more negative information. All this results in chronic stress and anxiety.

Basically, stress and reactivity engage the small mind which then turns off the bridge network, and essentially cuts off our access to the big mind.

Because our minds and bodies are deeply interconnected through our brain and its millions of neurons, even trivial thoughts that unconsciously pass through our minds will set off a chain of reactions throughout our neurobiology that impact virtually every cell in our brains and bodies.

Our cells are constantly watching our thoughts, which impact and change them nearly instantly.

Imagine a bowl the size of your skull filled with batteries continuously creating electrical impulses. This battery connects via millions of tiny wires to a large bag 3/4 filled with water – one of the most conductive elements in nature.

The water immediately absorbs every electrical impulse the batteries send, changing the water's molecular structure.

Similarly, when our brains circulate thoughts and emotions throughout our bodies, which are around 75 percent water, we become impacted even at the cellular level.

Again, we have the ability to control many situations and close negative feedback loops, such as by eating when hungry, or sleeping when tired.

However, we have little to no control over many other factors, such as the nature of our past and future, how others see us, our job security, how events should or shouldn't occur, unexpected illnesses, or time of our death, to name just a few.

The Brain Demands Control

The brain, charged with our survival, tries to do its job by continually keeping control of every internal and external element that it can.

Thus our sense of control, important to we humans but carrying no practical meaning in the real world, *originates in the brain.*

When we feel vulnerable, true or imagined, our desire to control increases and becomes more intense.

The absence of a sense of control, even though control is illusory, makes the brain agitated and the mind reactive.

Negative feedback loops open, distressing thoughts follow, and these keep us preoccupied during the day, awake at night, and generally exhausted and unproductive.

Open loops quietly overwhelm our nervous systems and drain our sense of liveliness and resiliency. They also deepen and spread our general stress level. We go from merely sensing stress to experiencing vulnerability and then fear.

The brain measures this fear second by second, and signals a state of true "emergency" linked to our survival to our mind.

So fear and reactivity penetrate our thoughts and emotions, and become a recurring habit. As a result more loops open and remain open, and stress becomes more intense. Our thoughts distort more deeply, and the stories we tell ourselves become gloomier.

This cycle quickly convinces us that our minds and bodies have come under attack by invisible, out-of-our-control forces.

This drawing shows what happens inside of us when we are under constant stress:

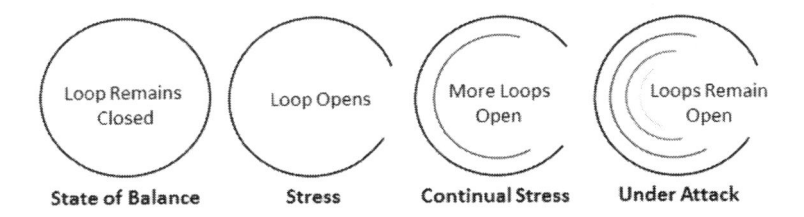

Loop Remains Closed	Loop Opens	More Loops Open	Loops Remain Open
State of Balance	**Stress**	**Continual Stress**	**Under Attack**

In the following chapters we will learn about specific ways in which the small mind opens endless negative loops which then distort our thoughts, and keep us feeling anxious and unsettled.

We will learn how to productively direct our thoughts, to close those loops, and in turn change our brains for the better in lasting ways.

The brain's ability to change itself is known as neuroplasticity. In essence the brain is plastic: flexible, changeable and adaptable, allowing the brain's neural structure and function to change with how we perceive, think, feel, and imagine. The brain's shaping and reshaping process is continuous; we do it intentionally or it will happen haphazardly. It is also bi-directional; it can shape and reshape in a productive fashion or vice versa.

When we decide to take charge, we practice *self-directed neuroplasticity and shape our brains in a productive way.*

"Anytime you're going to grow, you're going to lose something. You're losing what you're hanging onto to keep safe. You're losing habits that you're comfortable with, you're losing familiarity."

~ James Hillman

Seven

How Do We Know?

How do we know what we know, and experience and interact with ourselves, others and events in the world? And how do we make sense of them all?

Our *knowing* begins with our five senses – sight, hearing, touch, smell and taste (we use the first three most often) – which continually collect information from both our internal and external worlds, and send it as small electrical impulses to our brain, which processes and then forwards them.

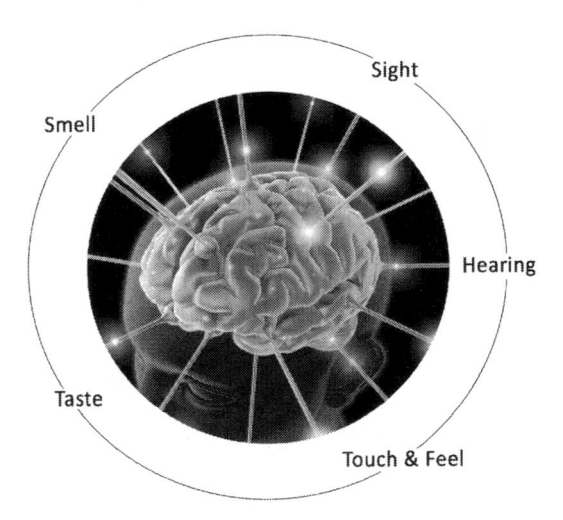

The intensity of our experience depends on the number and strength of the impulses we send to our brains. If we are walking across the street and a car is speeding toward us, our eyes send more and faster signals to our brain to force it to take action, such as having us walk faster or slower to avoid an accident.

When we relax and feel safe, and no immediate action is required, our senses send fewer signals to the brain and our relaxation deepens. This is what happens when we take a vacation from daily stimuli such as driving, working or taking care of others.

Let's look at what happens in the brain when the signals from our senses arrive, how they cause the mind to produce *thoughts*, and how that leads to our emotions and behaviors.

Upon arrival, the brain converts incoming information from the senses into electrical signals. These signals then release very small molecules, chemical messengers known as *neurotransmitters*, which carry them to various neurons within the brain.

Next, four regions of the brain – specific groups of neurons – get engaged to form our thoughts, emotions, memories and behaviors.

The sum of this internal brain activity is, as you'll recall, known as the mind.

The Four Regions of the Brain

Let's explore how these four brain regions interact and produce our perceptions, thoughts, emotions, memories and behavior.

The first region of the brain, known as the *thalamus,* takes delivery of incoming signals or information from our senses.

Its job is that of a traffic controller responsible for receiving and forwarding information related to what we need to accomplish. [64,65] It handles information including our voluntary physical movement, coordination, alertness and sleep.

It also forwards other types of information to a second region of the brain to define their emotional meaning.

The second region of the brain, the amygdala, is responsible for adding emotional interpretations to the signals the thalamus sends it. This region is like a painter who colors with emotions to the signals sent by the thalamus.

For that reason, I call the amygdala the *emotionizer.*

The *emotionizer* does its job by comparing the signals it is receiving to a large library of previous emotions stored in our long-term subconscious memory.[66,67] It acts extremely quickly so we can make appropriate emotional decisions to assure our safety. [68,69] This is how we instantly sense fear at the sight of a fire, an automobile too close to us, or excitement on seeing a loved one.

You recall from an earlier chapter that the *emotionizer* uses 2/3 of its capacity five times per second to look for negative information or signs of danger to protect our safety. **This makes the emotionizer our fear center.**

Two key points before we explore the next area of the brain:

First, since a thought impulse becomes an emotion at a blazingly fast speed, our emotions drive our behaviors and decisions. For example, when we decide to buy a car, we do research on every possible detail, and finally zero in on two models, which one do we buy? Nearly always the one that *feels* right.

We base our decisions on our emotions rather than logic. Therefore, **our emotions, not our thoughts or logic, primarily drive our decisions and behaviors.**

Second, since a thought impulse becomes an emotion nearly immediately after it enters the brain, *humans are primarily emotional rather than logical or rational beings*. This is the reason that *real and lasting change at the brain level happens only when we are able to productively shift our emotions.*

Back to the four regions of the brain.

The third region is called the Hippocampus, our memory system, which I call the *memorizer*. It is responsible for examining signals it receives from the emotionizer both for their emotional tone and for their spatial qualities. [70,71,72] For example, if someone stands uncomfortably close to me and stares me in the eye, the memorizer decides whether the nature of their gaze at that distance may pose a threat to me.

Based on its conclusion, the *memorizer* organizes this information and keeps it in either short or long-term memory, depending on the meaning and importance it attaches to it. If it concludes that I may be vulnerable, it considers that as a danger sign and stores it in long-term memory for future reference. On the hand, if it interprets the gaze as friendly and the distance comfortable, it stores the information in short-term memory since it poses no threat and is not useful for future reference.

Once the memorizer is done, it forwards the signal to another region of the brain known as the Hypothalamus.

Since this region is in charge of our hormonal system, I call it the brain's *pharmacy*.

This *pharmacy* bears a critical responsibility. It constantly monitors our vital functions including heart rate, blood pressure, circadian rhythm, temperature, weight, appetite, thirst, hunger, mood, sex drive, and sleeping and waking cycles. It does its job by directing our hormonal system to release or inhibit the secretion of specific hormones. This continually regulates and maintains our balance. [73,74,75]

For example, when we become stressed, it's because the *pharmacy*, as part of our stress-response, has delivered stress hormones such as adrenal and cortisol. When we feel relaxed, it is because the pharmacy has released dopamine as part of our relaxation response.

Both the release and inhibition of hormones influence our thoughts, emotions and behaviors. *The brain's pharmacy thus ultimately determines how we function physically and emotionally.*

While the activities of these four regions of the brain take place beyond our awareness, they all begin at a single point: our *sensory perceptions*. Our perceptions thus *ultimately* produce our thoughts, which in turn determine our emotions and behaviors.

This chart shows how the brain, step-by-step, turns our perceptions to our thoughts, emotions, memories and finally behaviors.

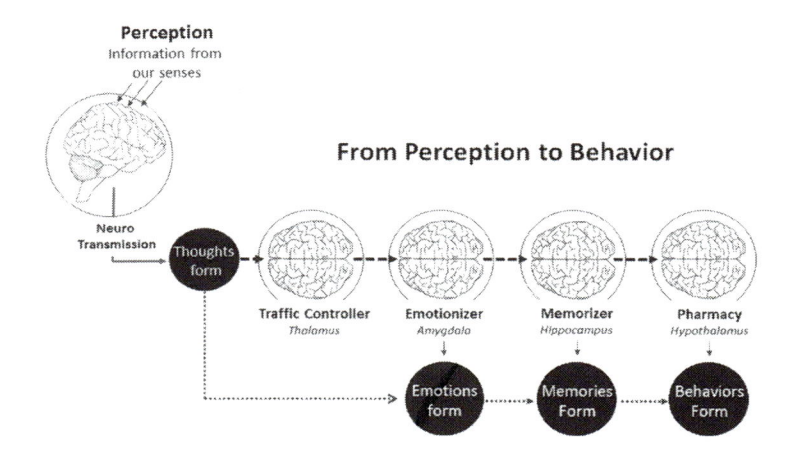

From Perception to Behavior

Perception — Information from our senses → Neuro Transmission → Thoughts form → Traffic Controller (*Thalamus*) → Emotionizer (*Amygdala*) → Memorizer (*Hippocampus*) → Pharmacy (*Hypothalamus*)

Thoughts form → Emotions form → Memories Form → Behaviors Form

What is Perception?

Our perceptions form by how we experience ourselves and the world around us. We recognize an apple by its round shape, sweet flavor and color, a song by its melody and the singer's voice, our feelings by how they influence our mind and bodies, a friend by his or her body shape, gestures and tone of voice, and our self by our facial features, height, weight and other characteristics.

Basically, we use the information we gather through our senses to create perceptions which lead us to recognize, interpret and then interact with ourselves, others and our environments in a meaningful way.

If how we perceive is colored by a *fearful mind,* our thoughts, emotions and behaviors follow, and the mind inevitably becomes unproductive – *the small mind experience.*

On the other hand, if our perceptions arise from a *calm natural mind*, our thoughts, emotions and behaviors similarly follow, and the mind becomes productive – *the big mind experience.*

But thoughts, despite the importance they carry, are fundamentally meaningless until we attach meaning to them.

Thoughts have no meaning until we attach one to them.

For example, we generally perceive red as a sign of caution or danger, and green as permission or relaxation. Neither has inherent meaning until we, having previously learned about colors, attach one to them. Through this process red becomes a color which carries a certain message, as does green.

Basically, *our perceptions form our thoughts, which determines our emotions and experiences.*

As biologist Dr. Bruce Lipton notes: *"The moment you change your perceptions, is the moment you rewrite the chemistry of your body."*

Thus, **how we perceive will ultimately leads us away or toward the life we want to live.**

Even though perceptions form our thoughts, we can more easily influence the thought process and skillfully direct it.

This in turn improves how we perceive. Let's look at how our thoughts are central to our experiences:

Thought:
Perception -> electrical impulses -> neurotransmission

Emotion:
Thoughts + meanings we attach to them

Belief:
Thoughts and emotions we deem true, regardless of evidence

Habit:
Thoughts + emotions + behaviors we often practice

Experience:
Lifelong learning

As we can see, our thoughts, moment-to-moment, generate our emotions, beliefs, habits and life experiences.

The following three drawings show the details of how, staring with thoughts, we generate our ways of being, doing and creating.

Our Way of Being
How we experience ourselves, and how others experience us.

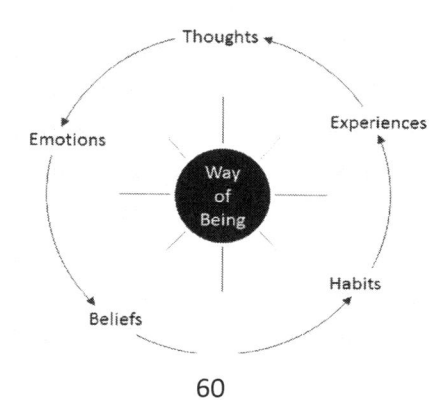

Our Way of Doing

How we express our Being in the world

Way of
Being
Intention
Way
of
Doing
Action
Behavior

Our Way of Creating

How our Being and Doing create the results we want.

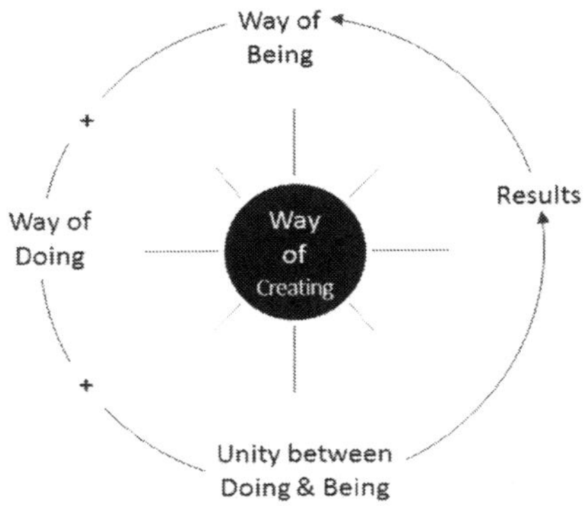
Way of
Being
+
Way of
Doing
Way
of
Creating
Results
+
Unity between
Doing & Being

As we can see, thoughts are central to shaping our ways of being, doing and creating.

Our thoughts therefore offer us a **single point of focus** through which we can improve *our ways of being, doing and creating at once.*

"If you correct your thoughts, the rest of your life will fall into place."

~ Lao Tzu

Eight

No Change Allowed

Is changing – doing away with old beliefs, improving behavior, putting the past behind us, and the like as easy as might seem from the outside?

Let's explore the brain's response when it faces change.

As you'll recall, the brain's every activity is aimed at protecting our safety, which takes priority over all others. For example, if we are involved in a car accident and have only the resources to either maintain consciousness or keep our heart pumping, the brain will promptly put us into a coma to maintain our blood flow and thus keep us alive.

The brain demands three things in exchange for protecting our survival: **balance**, **consistency** and **comfort**. Without them, *it becomes agitated and reactive.*

Why? Because the brain interprets any change or even an attempt at change as a potential threat to its balance, consistency and comfort. In other words, from the brain's perspective, change means risking our survival. It therefore becomes disturbed and wages war against the change.

Faced with the dilemma of change, the brain tries different ways to resolve its conflict quickly. It tries to persuade us by denying reality, creating self-doubt or engaging in procrastination. If not successful, it then creates resistance in increasing steps, which we experience as tension and even illness.

The brain's purpose for putting up such a fight is simple: *it is instinctively protecting our survival despite ourselves.*

Research shows that the failure rate in making any meaningful change is up to 90 percent. The reason is that the brain which is at home with balance, consistency and comfort *starts building resistance to our efforts to change around ½ second before we make up our minds.* [76]

Let's explore this further, since we have all attempted to bring some level of change to our lives, with little or no long-term success.

The brain starts resisting change by creating tension and imbalances throughout our minds and bodies. As a result, negative feedback loops open up and the *emotionizer* steps in to help the brain reestablish its demands. We experience and interpret the tension as self-doubt, anxiety, vulnerability and ultimately fear, all of which lead us to abandon our efforts to change over time.

When we experience those intense emotions we begin to question the rationale for stepping out of our comfort zones into the unfamiliar, *which is what real change requires.*

This questioning stirs our deeper concerns about our survival we hold in the subconscious memory.

The small mind combines these concerns with memories of our past failures, attaches those to our efforts to change, and fills our minds with discouraging yet convincing thoughts and stories as to why we cannot succeed this time either.

How do we experience all of this? Often as an inner voice whispering: Back off. Be careful. Go slow. Compromise. Get real. Don't trust yourself. Why put yourself through all this? What if? Value others' opinions more than your own. *In short, we generate a deep and convincing sense of self-doubt and insecurity.*

As a result, more negative loops open, tension and imbalance increase intolerably, and we generate the experience of being under attack. Inner strength wanes and backing off starts looking like a more sensible choice than moving ahead.

Then the small mind creates new beliefs to relieve, if only temporarily, the emotional discomfort from backing off: *It wasn't meant to be. What else could I do? It wasn't really that bad. Luck wasn't on my side. I just don't have what it takes.* And my personal favorite: *Everything happens for the best.*

The brain, having won its fight to regain balance, consistency and comfort, backs off, and the open loops close. We in turn retreat back to our comfort zones and our previous habitual ways of being, doing and creating, even if less than desirable or successful.

The brain then adds its "win" to our subconscious memories for future use should we attempt to change again.

What are we to do? Are we forever stuck with these unhelpful patterns?

Certainly not.

As you recall, *meaningful change happens only when we can productively shift our emotions, which leads to lasting reshaping of the brain.*

So the question is: How do we shift our mind from its protective, resistant mode to its learning, adapting and evolving mode – the one which naturally supports our desire to make progress – without needless anxiety?

Our Option

We can take the easy road by exercising our option to move ourselves to the big mind again and again. In doing so, we bypass the small mind's restraints, and benefit from abilities inherent in the big mind.

How? As you'll recall, *we can run only one mind at a time.* By using the exercise on page 32, you can switch off the small mind, turn on the big mind, and have it as your primary ally in your advancement.

Practice in shifting from the small mind to the big mind is vital to establish fresh neural pathways and connections in the brain. These then reinforce the change we desire at the thought, emotional and behavioral levels, and imprint on the brain.

This is brain neuroplasticity in action, now with you in charge.

The simplicity and ease of this process will become more apparent in the following chapters.

Nine

Why Do We Do That?

Research reveals that we have around 70,000 thoughts on average per day.[77] Long the subject of rigorous scientific investigation, research on influence of thoughts indicates that 75 to 98 percent of all types of illnesses are directly tied to our thoughts. [78,79,80,81,82,83,84,85,86,87,88]

Other research estimates that a staggering 85 percent of several mental and physical diseases, as well as 75 to 90 percent of visits to physicians, are related to stress. [89,90]

The World Health Organization and the International Agency for Research on Cancer report that around 80 percent of cancers are due to lifestyles rather than genetic factors. [91]

Similarly, research [92] reveals that only 5 percent of cancer and cardiovascular cases are related to patients' hereditary factors.

A 2015 joint study by Harvard and Stanford Universities found that workplace stress causes at least 120,000 deaths each year. Factors directly related to this include *perceptions of "unfairness," "lack of control"* and *"job insecurity."* [93]

And not surprisingly, the latest scientific research has found a direct link between stress and the weakening of our immune systems. [94,95,96]

The Thinking Process

The thinking process, through which we create such far-reaching impact in our minds and bodies, occurs automatically. *It simply appears in our minds and we then become aware of it.*

If asked how we speak, we'll commonly answer that we push air through our mouths and combine it with sound to form words. However, if asked how we think, there is no obvious explanation.

Yet thinking takes up the largest part of our time. Conversations about thoughts, ideas and ideals dominate much of human activity.

The French philosopher Descartes declared *thinking* to be the core of our existence when he stated: *"I think, therefore I am."* What he is saying is that *we know that we exist through our thoughts.*

We can easily see the influence of thinking. Millions of lives have been, and continue to be, lost over ideological differences. At the same time, life-saving discoveries have been achieved through creative thinking. All of these have started and ended with a thought – a very small drop of liquid chemical on a nerve ending within the skull.

Why Do We Think in the First Place?

Why do we think? Because *thinking is a tool* crucial to taking care of our basic survival needs, such as securing food, shelter and clothing. Thinking also helps us establish our identities – the combination of our personality traits, features, education, skills and occupation – with which we make our way in the world.

Once our identity forms we use thinking to create internal maps to help us find our place in the world, make sense of what is happening to us and around us. Our maps also help us learn what to do and not to do, and how to fit in with family, friends, and coworkers.

How do we know what we are thinking? We tell ourselves through self-talk about the content of our thoughts. We constantly talk internally and use that conversation to tell ourselves how to behave in ways that are most beneficial to our survival and happiness.

All in all, thinking is a survival tool for taking care of our needs.

If we had no needs, there would be no reason for thinking. And our thinking becomes more involved and intense when we attempt to satisfy more than our basic survival needs.

For example, if we get hungry in the normal course of the day, our thoughts remain calm until the usual time to eat arrives. However, if we perceive ourselves to be famished, and our survival possibly compromised, our thoughts will become more involved and intense.

In other words, thoughts about what we *must* have are more intense and engulfing than *routine thoughts*. And the intensity of 'must have' thoughts is what produces stress and anxiety.

Needs are, of course, a natural part of human life. But the tendency to constantly want more, or never-ending needs, eventually produces unhappiness.

This is called the *Hedonistic Treadmill* – the tendency to constantly grasp for "more and better" which lessens happiness at each successive step.

As St. Augustine observed centuries ago: *"A true saying it is, Desire hath no rest, is infinite in itself, endless, and as one calls it, a perpetual rack, or horse-mill."*

If that is the case, why do so many of us center our lives on going after "more and better" despite not really needing it?

That striving comes from wanting to satisfy one or more of our false thoughts about what we supposedly need. As a result, any satisfaction we gain is at best temporary.

As Henry David Thoreau expressed it: *"A man is rich in proportion to the number of things he can afford to let alone."*

Thinking about Thinking

Our advanced human neocortex gives us not only the *power to think* but also *the ability to reflect,* or *think about our thoughts.*

For example, if involved in a car accident, we typically reflect on the incident, holding an internal conversation such as *why and how it happened, whose fault it was,* and *how much worse it could have been.*

The ability to reflect also allows us reexamine our thoughts, fine tune them, discard them, or keep them as they were.

We can use our ability to reflect as an asset by learning how to use it productively in service of creativity, refining ideas, and accomplishing overall learning.

However, when our minds become reactive, our thinking becomes distorted, negative thoughts become repetitive and this prolongs our anxiety and reactivity. The mind automatically becomes unproductive.

Inside the Brain

What happens inside the brain when the mind becomes agitated and thus reactive?

This is the process: Our senses gather information and send it to the brain's *traffic* controller, which then forwards it on to the *emotionizer,* which checks with long-term memory for a match to determine the signal's *emotional tone.*

If a match is not found, it considers the signal new information, and turns to the neocortex, home to the big mind, for instruction on how to best handle it.

The big mind then sends "rational" instructions to the *emotionizer*, the other regions act accordingly, and we *appropriately respond.*

However, the *emotionizer's* response changes dramatically when it finds an emotional match in our memories, a previous incident that in anyway was recorded a threat, actual or not, to our safety.

In that case it decides that a similar undesirable situation is reoccurring now, and must be stopped *immediately.* It considers that time is of the essence, that allowing access to our rational thinking will waste valuable time, and will interfere with the action needed to protect our safety.

The *emotionizer* therefore orders the *brain's pharmacy* to deliver adrenal hormone to the neocortex, where rational thinking is formed, and *cut our access to it.*

So the brain processes emotional information that signifies potential danger *milliseconds faster* than it processes rational information. [97,98] Thus our objectivity and rationality quickly give way to reactivity – our fight, flight or freeze response.

This entire process arises from our survival instinct.

Say that the *emotionizer* becomes alarmed by a fast approaching car. The brain doesn't want us to stand in the middle of the road contemplating what may happen. Rather, it wants us to react instantly and do something such as running forward or moving backward to avert injury.

When we are *actually* threatened, this appropriate reactivity saves our lives. The loops the *emotionizer* opened now close, because we are safe.

However, when distorted thoughts concerning *nonexistent threats* make the mind agitated and reactive, we act irrationally and at times destructively to protect ourselves. The negative feedback loops thus remain open, more distortions arise in our minds and we become increasingly anxious and reactive.

In section 2 we will more deeply explore how the ways we understand and make sense of information – our cognition processes – shape our reactivity, and how to free ourselves from them.

Section 2

In previous chapters we gained a practical understanding of how our brains and minds work and how they impact us.

We learned about the roles the small mind and the big mind play in creating our life experiences.

We have seen that we experience productivity, creativity and satisfaction when the two minds harmoniously work together. And how, when they do not, we experience anxiety, stress, ineptness and even illness.

We also learned that only one of these minds can be active at any given time – when the small mind is active, the big mind shuts off, and vice versa.

In the chapters that follow, we will explore the cognitive processes that engage the small mind and how, through four specific modes of thinking, the small mind creates limiting forces that block us from using our big mind, and progressing in our lives.

Going forth, I will refer to these four modes of thinking as the *four negative mind-characters.* I call them 'characters' to differentiate them from other thinking modes.

We've already learned how to switch off the small mind by using our senses to tap into our big mind.

Next we will learn how to quiet the small mind's four negative characters by using simple practical tools.

I suggest that you set aside time to complete the exercises that appear at the end of chapters. Doing them the *first thing in the morning* will help you integrate your new learning into practical doing each day at home and at work.

If you are reading an electronic version of this book, use a note book for doing the exercises.

As you complete these practices by writing down your responses and insights, you will build skills you can use in **all** areas of your life.

These skills will then become your guide, helping you to remove whatever is blocking your path to your big mind.

Let's begin.

Ten

The Cast of Characters

In chapter four we explored our cognitive networks in detail, and the roles each play in how we experience and lead our lives.

In this section we will explore how the small mind gets entrenched and the specific ways in which it unhealthily impacts our ways of being, doing and creating.

As you'll recall, the small mind activates when the brain gets agitated. But how does the small mind sustain itself? The following factors enable it:

- The first factor is the brain's **Negativity Bias**, facilitated by the emotionizer, which uses 2/3 of its capacity five times per second to constantly search for negative information. [97]

- The second factor is **Selective Attention**, our ability to choose *what to pay attention to and what to ignore when they occur at the same time.* This ensures that the brain will select and react faster to *any* information that concerns our survival and safety. [98]

For instance, when a car is fast approaching we prioritize that event over looking at someone crossing the street wearing a nice jacket.

Selective Attention restricts our attention to only one message at a time so we don't become overwhelmed with the large volume of information our senses pour into our brains.[99] It is believed that we are conscious of 10 percent of that volume. The other 90 percent processed without our conscious awareness. This is still a large volume of information, as we have around 70,000 thoughts per day.

Negativity Bias, Selective Attention and the emotionizer interplay and enable each other in powerful ways.

As you recall, the emotionizer continually collects negative information, producing the brain's Negativity Bias. The memorizer then absorbs and stores that information to make it quickly and easily accessible to us when we need it.

Selective Attention then forces the brain to consider negative data as priority survival information, ignore irrelevant data, and engage the brain's other regions to fend of potential danger. [100]

This activates the last region of the brain, the pharmacy, to release stress hormones into our bodies to prepare us to react – the fight, flight or freeze response.

This cycle is how the mind becomes reactive, bombards our thought stream with negative information and distorts them, and warps our perception.

- The third factor, the ***Illusion-of-Truth*** effect, is our tendency to *believe that to which we are exposed most frequently*. [101] This includes the things that frequently passes through our minds. When the same thoughts and stories keep repeating again and again, we, regardless of their authenticity, believe them.

All else being equal, we will buy products, invest in stocks, go to places, socialize with people and engage in behaviors we've been most frequently exposed to in the past.

We store the information we are most often exposed in long-term subconscious memory. This allows us to act on it without conscious effort. *This is how we develop habits and comfort zones.*

Subconscious memory is also where we store our beliefs, especially those regarding survival.[102,103] Therefore when thoughts of being vulnerable keep circulating in the mind, we get pushed to act, often without conscious awareness or discretion, to protect ourselves.

Reacting appropriately is of course justified when we face real danger. However, when *illusion-of-truth* convinces us of a nonexistent danger, our resulting behavior negatively impacts ourselves, others and the world around us.

The *illusion-of-truth* explains **why we accept our distorted thoughts as true regardless of their authenticity**.

As the renowned American psychologist William James put it: *"There is nothing so absurd that it cannot be believed as truth if repeated often enough."*

When distorted thoughts take center stage in our minds, and we are unable to distinguish fact from fiction, we begin to give those thoughts credibility and authority.

We then start believing and acting, almost automatically, on whatever thoughts pass through our minds. Our behavior forms a close union with our misleading thoughts, and soon enough, *our life experience becomes about whatever last thought passed through our minds.*

Soon we end up believing that we are actually our thoughts.

We then try to use the same *distorted* thoughts to address our challenges. But as Einstein aptly noted: *"We cannot solve our problems with the same level of thinking that created them."*

It simply does not work, since a thought, just like a tree that cannot see itself, cannot distinguish itself from other thoughts, especially when distorted. It instead gets tangled up in its own distortions, and creates more of them.

As we discussed earlier, we use our thoughts to develop ideas about who we are, what we are capable of, how loveable we are, how we fit in, and how to make our ways in the world.

When we apply distorted thoughts to those tasks, this warped set of impressions creates convincing illusions and beliefs about us not being good enough, capable enough or loveable enough – as well as being separated, limited and stuck.

This creates convincing illusions and beliefs about **WHO WE ARE NOT**.

These beliefs soon take root and begin feeding our perceptions. Our perceptions form our thoughts, which in turn shape our emotions and behaviors. Therefore *in believing who we are not, our entire sense of self as well as our views becomes warped.*

As Anais Nin eloquently put it, *"We don't see the world as it is, we see it as we are."*

A great story illustrates this point.

Socrates had gone for a walk outside the city walls of Athens. He was taking a rest, sitting on a milepost on the road around five miles from the city, when a traveler approached along the road.

"Greetings, friend! Can you tell me, is this the road to Athens?" Socrates assured him it was. "Carry straight on ahead. It's a big city. You can't miss it."

"Tell me," asked the traveler, "what are the people of Athens like?" "Well," said Socrates, "tell me where you're from, and what the people there are like, and I'll tell you about the people of Athens."

"I'm from Argos. And I am proud and happy to tell you that the people of Argos are the friendliest, happiest, most generous people you could ever wish to meet."

"And I'm very happy to tell you, my friend," said Socrates, "that the people of Athens are exactly the same."

A few moments passed and another traveler approached. "Greetings, friend! Can you tell me, is this the road to Athens?" Socrates assured him it was.

"Tell me," said the traveler, "what are the people of Athens like?" "Well," said Socrates, "tell me where you're from, and what the people there are like, and I'll tell you about the people of Athens."

"I'm from Argos. And I am sad and disappointed to tell you that the people of Argos are the meanest, most miserable and least friendly people you could ever wish to meet."

"And I'm very disappointed to tell you, my friend," said Socrates, "that the people of Athens are exactly the same."

Carl Jung beautifully illustrates the essence of this story in saying: *"We meet ourselves time and time again in thousand disguises on the path of life."*

The point: just as beliefs and perceptions go hand in hand, so do perceptions and expectations. They're three points on a revolving circle, each feeding the other.

And thus we notice more of that which we expect to see. **And this begins with ourselves.**

We must become aware of this tendency to let our perceptions guide us continually toward more of the same, and instead actively seek fresh ways of perceiving. Otherwise, our distorted perceptions will lead us to *noticing more of who we are not*.

As Wayne Dyer put it: *"If you change the way you look at things, the things you look at change."* **Again, this includes ourselves.**

With this understanding of how the small mind gets entrenched, let's now explore the specific ways in which it sustains itself, and circulates its restraining forces through its four negative characters.

The Four Negative Mind-Characters

I have named these four thinking modes of the small mind the negative mind-characters. I refer to them as *characters* because, unbeknownst to us they slip in and become part of our personhood, distort our thoughts, adversely impact our emotions, and misdirect our behaviors.

These characters use the small mind's *past-and-future* orientation to generate obsessive thinking, insecurity, mistrust and self-doubt. These qualities make us rigid, protective and limit our ability to learn, develop and grow.

The impressions they imprint on our minds are largely based on fear. Linked to our survival instincts, they appear real much of the time.

The four negative characters act together with snowballing effect. When one activates and is not quieted in a timely manner, the next one goes off, and so on.

However, if we quiet the first character as it emerges, the others will not engage, and we'll avoid their damaging impact altogether.

In the next four chapters you will learn the specific ways in which these negative mind-characters take over our minds, and how to overcome them.

Keep in mind, however, that these mind-characters do not represent any kind of mental sickness; **they are rather the children of thoughts distorted by fear.**

Since fear plays a central role in distorting our thoughts, let's explore it thoroughly.

What is Fear? Simply put, *fear is our resistance to vulnerability*.

Whenever we feel emotionally or physically vulnerable, our survival instinct drives us to naturally resist potential danger and to protect our safety. This resistance produces the emotion we call fear.

Fear is what sustains the four negative mind-characters.

How? Most of us have been indoctrinated to believe that fear is a good motivator. That we can get things done, succeed, and better protect ourselves through *fearing* than through confidence. Being fearful is considered as being realistic.

As early as our childhoods, we hear that if we don't do certain things do we'll end up being nobodies.

And multiple studies confirm that we learn more from, and are motivated more by, negative reinforcements than positive ones. Basically, fear and fearing has over time become the fabric of, and operating principle of our minds.

Therefore we come to believe that fear offers us the best defense against perceived physical or emotional vulnerability. *But in fearing, we activate the four negative mind-characters which makes us feel even more vulnerable and fearful.*

We constantly get caught in that unhelpful paradox enabled by our natural survival instinct.

Freeing ourselves from these ingrained habitual fears requires vigilance and practice.

How to Overcome Fear

This book offers simple practices at the end of several chapters that allow us to turn our knowledge of how those mind-characters create our fears, build specific skills to effectively quiet them, and thus overcome the fears they instill.

Building skills is key because pure knowledge is fleeting until we can apply it through doing.

You will be best served by putting what you learn here into practice through the exercises provided.

Using them as tools you will build the essential skills necessary to recognize the four negative mind-characters and how to quiet them down.

Space is provided in the book to do the exercises in the next four chapters. I also suggest having a small notebook handy throughout the day so you can jot down your related thoughts. This will both raise your awareness and build your skills.

In the next chapter we will explore the first negative mind-character.

"The key to growth is the introduction of higher dimensions of consciousness into our awareness."

~ Lao Tzu

Eleven

The Reacter

The first negative mind-character consists of an internal emotional mechanism called a Reacter. It acts as the brain's defense system and moves into self-protection mode when it senses that our physical or emotional well-being might be in danger.

The Reacter switches on in the presence of what we call triggers. Triggers in general include unpleasant emotional experiences such as incidents that cause emotional distress or trauma. We can also get triggered when we perceive ourselves being criticized, blamed, controlled, disrespected or treated unjustly. When any of these surface, we become emotionally uneven, lose good judgment, and react in irrational and often self-defeating ways.

Importantly, the Reacter is the doorkeeper to the other three negative mind-characters which you will learn about in the following chapters. Once the Reacter gets triggered, so do the other three characters.

So once we learn to recognize our triggers and not to react to them, we avoid the influence of the other negative mind-characters as well.

In the Nervous System

When we perceive a potential physical or emotional threat and feel vulnerable, whether real or as a thought, memory or even imagination, the brain releases stress hormones into our system to prepare for our self-defense. The first thing those hormones do is to cut off the lines of communication to our rational thinking, which takes place in the neocortex region. Therefore, we lose objectivity, and involuntarily act hurriedly and often irrationally to fend off the perceived danger. Under ongoing pressure, including work- or home-related stress, illness, trauma, emotional challenges and fear, the brain releases stress hormones nearly constantly. Getting triggered over even the smallest incidents begins to feel normal and then becomes habitual.

Types of Triggers

The Reacter gets triggered primarily by how we perceive and interpret our inner world, such as our thoughts, stories, memories, imagining, stress, exhaustion, disappointments, etc.

Even though we get triggered by our interactions with the outside world, including co-workers, family members, friends or the weather, it is in how we perceive and interpret those events that causes us to get triggered.

Sometimes we can even get triggered about having gotten triggered. For example, we get upset about having been upset or even sick. Regardless of whether our experiences are formed by outside or internal events, it is *how we perceive our thoughts and emotions* about them, and the *meanings we attach* to them that determines our reactivity or rational response.

Spotting the Reacter

The thoughts and emotions that activate our triggers reside in the subconscious memory. Therefore *when triggered we tend to react impulsively, because we are unaware of their source.*

When the Reacter engages, we feel an unpleasant energetic shift in our minds and bodies. The body gets tense and certain muscles get tight, breath gets short and the heart starts pounding faster. The mind races and becomes disorganized and chaotic. Internal pressure to act quickly builds. The brain is readying the body to fight off perceived danger and vulnerability to regain balance as quickly as possible.

What We Do

We typically react in one of the following ways:

1. **Fight**, based on the perception that we will win;

2. **Flight**, based on the perception that we will lose, or

3. **Freeze**, to gauge the situation and decide which of the first two is better for us

Let's look at examples of what we typically *do* in each of these three cases:

- Fight: Manipulating, deceiving, demanding control, fault finding, threatening, verbal/physical aggression, criticizing, back stabbing and gossiping.

- Flight: Falsely agreeing, going along, giving up, playing aloof, silent treatment, acting distant or formal, playing nice, physically or emotionally leaving the scene.
- Freeze: Confusion, pleading, begging for time, becoming physically or emotionally immobile.

Each method is designed to help us *gain control* over the situation *as quickly as possible* and protect our physical and emotional well-being.

But *acting on a trigger creates emotional imbalance*, which opens consecutive negative loops that remain open. As a result, toxic hormones constantly release into the mind and body, we become even more reactive, and further enable the small mind. The net result is damaging short and long-term behavior. If allowed to continue, this counterproductive behavior will lead to even more self-defeating outcomes.

Acting on a trigger creates emotional imbalance which agitates the mind.

How to Quiet the Reacter

Quieting our Reacter is crucial to successfully escaping from the chain of distressing experiences that inevitably follow when the other negative mind-characters engage.

As mentioned earlier, our *Reacter is the doorway to the other three mind-characters.* By learning to quiet our Reacter in time, we sidestep the fight/flight/freeze mode. Responding replaces reacting, allowing us to behave in balanced ways to generate the results we want.

Recognizing our Triggers is the Key

Reactivity points to our holding distorted thoughts somewhere beyond our conscious awareness. We become reactive when some stimulus triggers those thoughts. The first step toward recognizing in advance how we get triggered and what we do leads us to respond in a functional way rather than react.

We all have personal triggers which represent our specific needs. Remember that *needs are not bad; some serve us well*. The need to be treated respectfully is an honorable one. But becoming enslaved to our needs, and reacting whenever we perceive them not being met, is a condition from which we want to free ourselves.

Needs are natural human desires as long as they don't control us and make us reactive when we don't get them.

Watch for signs that lead to reactivity. For example, if something is triggering your anxiety, anger or sadness, *learn to identify the signs that lead up to it.* Becoming aware of what to watch for lets us to nip it in the bud early on.

As Victor Frankl noted: "*Between stimulus and response there is a space. In that space is our power to choose our response. In our response lies our growth and our freedom."*

Practice

The first step in the process of Self-mastery is to recognize and start managing our Triggers. The following practice will help you to build the skill to do that.

From the following list choose 5 needs which are most important to you, and which most often set off your emotions when you believe they might not be met.

I get triggered when I ***don't get*** or ***don't think I will get***....

☐ Acceptance   ☐ Attention   ☐ Understanding

☐ Control   ☐ Feeling safe   ☐ Feeling valued

☐ Respect   ☐ Love   ☐ Treated fairly

☐ Feeling included   ☐ Peace of mind   ☐ Trust

☐ Comfort   ☐ Order   ☐ Balance

☐ Freedom   ☐ Affection   ☐ Consistency

☐ Approval   ☐ Feeling liked   ☐ Compassion

Others: (list your own)

☐ _____   ☐ _____   ☐ _____

☐ _____   ☐ _____   ☐ _____

Next, read slowly through your selections and notice sensations such as agitation, shutting down, chaos, uneasiness, sadness, or the force of fight/flight/freeze activity.

For *each selection*, write 1 for the lowest level of mind/body tension you notice and 5 for the highest level next to it.

Next, select your three triggers starting with the *highest* score from the above chart and write them on the next page.

1. _____
2. _____
3. _____

For *each of those triggers* answer these questions, especially when concerning important people or situations in your life. Be very specific and thorough.

A. From whom (or in what areas) do I want to get it? (Example: *I want praise from my partner/parents/boss.*)

1. _____
2. _____
3. _____

B. What do I do to get it? (*I keep doing things that he/she likes hoping he/she would do the same for me.*)

1. _____
2. _____
3. _____

C. Exactly how do I want to get it? (*I want to be told, I want to get a gift, I want to be held.*)

1. _____
2. _____
3. _____

D. How do I react when you don't get it? (*I become angry, withdraw and treat him/her less than respectfully.*)

1. _____
2. _____
3. _____

You just completed an important step in recognizing and side-stepping your triggers and reactivity.

What did I learn from doing this exercise? Be specific.

_____

_____

How can you use this learning in your daily life? Be specific.

_____

_____

Daily Practice

Throughout the day, notice whenever an unpleasant energetic shift tenses your mind and body and creates internal pressure to react quickly. If so, an emotional trigger has fired up and your Reacter has stepped in.

Immediately ask yourself what are you **not getting**? You answer lies behind what has triggered you.

Then review how you reacted. How you feel about your reaction? How beneficial was the outcome?

Remember: the small mind has the strong ability to self-justify. For example, it will justify an unhelpful reaction by convincing you that "he/she deserved it," "that situation called for it," "I had to put my foot down" or "it's the best I could do under the circumstances."

Intentionally decide to pay no attention to the small mind's excuses, even if they seem justified. This excuse strategy is just how it prevents you from looking deeply into its inner workings because that will strip it of its control.

Learning how to quiet the Reacter begins with awareness of how we get triggered, and this provides the quickest path to freeing ourselves from its damaging effects.

It's up to you.

In the next chapter, we will discuss the next negative mind-character, the Ruler, how it behaves and how it influences us, and how to quiet it as well.

"A quiet mind is all you need. All else will happen rightly, once your mind is quiet."

~ Nisargadatta

Twelve

The Ruler

The second negative mind-character, after the Reacter, is our internal Ruler. This character keeps making up rules which we experience as thoughts about how we, others, conditions and the world *should or shouldn't be*.

How the Ruler Rules

Our daily lives present us with challenges which cannot be avoided or ignored. But when we invent rules about how we "should or shouldn't" be, we add a lot of self-criticism and unnecessary stress and anxiety to our already complex lives.

And when we assign those "should or shouldn't" rules to other people, and endless numbers of situations, we create frustration, mistrust, disconnection, judgment and many other needless complexities.

Confucius, the Chinese philosopher and thinker, captured this human tendency in saying: *"Life is really simple, but we insist on making it complicated."*

When the rules we invent are not *fulfilled exactly* the way we want them to be, our Ruler becomes frustrated, agitated and then activated.

As you recall, the four negative mind-characters set each other off beneath our awareness. *It all begins when the Ruler becomes unhappy and triggers the Reacter.* This happens, for instance, when we don't get the respect we believe we *should* get, and more generally, whenever our rules are not met to our satisfaction.

It all begins when our Ruler becomes frustrated by not getting its rules met, and triggers the Reacter.

Unmasking the Ruler

We can recognize our rules by paying close attention to the language we use; for example, words such as *should, shouldn't, must* or *mustn't*. We semi-consciously say things to ourselves like: "I *should* have known better." "He *shouldn't* treat me like that." "The world *ought* to be a better place."

When the Ruler activates, we notice sensations of tension, agitation, uneasiness, shutting down, and perhaps even rigidity in our minds and bodies.

Behind the Scenes

The Ruler establishes itself in two ways. First, it offers us a sense of control and authority, which we readily accept since we link those to the ability to protect our survival.

But this is misleading since constant and uncontrollable change is the natural law that governs the universe in which we live. In reality we cannot control let alone know what will happen to us even a few minutes from now. *We can predict, but we cannot control.*

Thus we set ourselves up for constant conflict with a reality that is neither predictable nor controllable.

Second, the Ruler offers to alleviate this conflict for us. We readily accept that offer too since our brains demand balance, and we crave inner peace.

By creating convincing illusions that we'll have control and inner peace, the Ruler guarantees its influence in our lives.

We easily buy into the illusions the Ruler instills in us, and thus become its servant in meeting its 'should and shouldn't' demands. We give in to fight/flight/freeze reactions by turning angry, silent, persuasive, loving, charming, blaming, or withdrawn when we don't get our rules met. We assume that manipulating will help us get our way and ease our conflict. This is another false notion, because we inevitably create more unease in trying to get our shoulds and shouldn'ts met.

The Ruler hides itself by convincing us that inventing rules is a wise trait; the sign of a "caring" person. My believing that you *should* or *shouldn't* act in a certain way means that I care about you and your happiness.

This is of course false, and only the Ruler's covert way to exert control.

But the small mind's expertise to self-justify keeps the Ruler in place.

Rules versus Plans

It is important to understand the difference between rules, in comparison to plans and expectations, as they are very different.

Plan and expectations are natural and healthy human desires, such as wanting to be happy, peaceful, loved and successful.

However, when we become *rigid* about our plans or expectations, and *not getting them met becomes a serious issue*, we have effectively *turned them into rules*.

For example, when I expect to be loved in a particular relationship, and find that I am not, I become disappointed and may decide to explore other options, including a conversation with my partner.

My *unmet expectation* has me look for and act on getting other doors open.

When, however, I turn being loved into a rigid rule, and don't get exactly what I imagined I *should* get, I become devastated, reactive and stuck.

My unmet rules push me to actions and behaviors which ultimately don't serve me well.

Remembering this difference between expectations and rules accomplishes two important things. First, we begin to distinguish our Ruler from other mind characters. This aids us in moving forward in functional ways to achieve our goals. Second, this will *quiet the Ruler and curb its damaging influence.*

How to Identify the Ruler

To identify the Ruler, watch for these signs:

1. Using words such as *should, shouldn't, must* or *mustn't* to yourself, others or events.

2. The small mind trying to convince you that:

   - You *should* look for answers and direction outside of yourself, and

   - You *should* trust others, especially those you consider authorities, more than yourself.

   - Becoming reactive is a normal response, even helpful to get what you want.

Once you notice any of the above signs, the Ruler has stepped in and is creating illusions of control and authority. Remind yourself that **the Ruler, and not the people or situations in your life,** is the true cause of your unhappiness.

This understanding is key to freeing yourself from rules and judgments that your Ruler levies against you and others.

Our rules, not people or conditions in our life, is the true cause of our reactivity and unhappiness.

Comparing and Contrasting

It's important to understand how the brain and the Ruler feed each other. This is how: The brain naturally functions by comparing and contrasting. For example, when I see a yellow color, my brain compares it with similar shades of yellow I have seen in the past and stored in my memory, and thus decides what shade of yellow I am looking at now.

The Ruler also uses comparing and contrasting to invent rules.

If I say to myself "my food *should* taste better" or "I *should* be more successful," I am in fact comparing the taste of the food in front of me, or my degree of existing success, to some kind of a model or standard I believe is better. Without making these *should* rules, I have no basis for making comparisons and thus judgments.

Let's consider another example. When I make up a rule that I *should* be better than I am now, I have a standard in mind; someone I perceive as better, whom I *should* become more like. In reality, though, I have no idea whether that comparison is realistic or even suitable to me. In doing so I am in fact *making up a fantasy, and pursuing it as a rule.*

The Ruler's Method

The Ruler's strategy for making up rules is to attach the core values of *good, bad, right* and *wrong* to our thoughts. The values we have attached combined with the brain's natural compare/contrast mode becomes the method with which we form judgments.

Our judgments are expressions of our unmet rules.

Without such judgments, we become free to develop ourselves in beneficial ways. We build stronger relationships with others.

Thus we will, by intentionally refraining from attaching arbitrary values of *good, bad, right* and *wrong* to our thoughts and emotions, function far more naturally, productively and be able to maintain healthier relationships.

The following practice will help you to build the skill to do that.

Practice

Write your answer under each column. Be specific.

How I am Now	How I should/shouldn't, must/mustn't be	Compared to whom?
I am an ok partner	I should be better	My ... whose relationship lasted 30 years

Do the same for three people you consider important in your life. Use the same three columns:

How is my partner/coworker/ family now	How he/she/they should/shouldn't, be	Compared to whom?
He/she is not that responsible	He/she should accept more responsibility	

What have you learned in doing these exercises?

_____

_____

How can you use this learning in your daily life? Be specific.

_____

_____

Daily Practice

As you go about your day, pay attention to how you use Ruler's words such as *should, shouldn't, must* and *mustn't* applied to yourself, others and events, even in the smallest way. Ask yourself *how you want yourself and others to be different*. Use that understanding to step back and quiet the Ruler.

Awareness of patterns is the quickest path to freeing yourself from your Ruler.

It's up to you.

In the next chapter, we will discuss the next negative mind-character, the Damager, and how to quiet that one as well.

"There is a huge amount of freedom that comes to you when you take nothing personally."

~ Miguel Ruiz

Thirteen

The Damager

The third negative mind-character, after the Reacter and Ruler, is the Damager. When the Ruler's *shoulds* and *shouldn'ts* are not met, the Reacter triggers, and it signals the Damager to step in.

We are now seeing how when one character activates, it automatically engages the others.

The Damager in Action

The Damager uses the Ruler's frustration over our failing to measure up to its should and shouldn't rules to make us feel not enough using different disguises: incapable, unworthy, unlovable, guilty and ashamed.

In doing so, t*he Damager gives us the false impression that we are damaged or broken within for failing to meet the Ruler's subjective benchmarks*. But these are false feelings since the Damager, like the Ruler, is a product of the distorted thoughts.

The Damager creates three thinking/feeling states to express its false impressions to us:

1. I am not *good* enough

2. I am not *capable* enough

3. I am not *loveable* enough

In general, **I am not... enough**, with us filling the gap depending on what kind of challenge we are facing.

The Damager tries to convince us that we are "not enough" by many methods, but its underlying message remains the same: *we are broken or damaged within.*

And to make its message more believable, the Damager brings up every past challenge we have stored in our subconscious memories, labels them as "failures," and reminds us of them every time we want to step out of our habitual ways to change our ways of being, doing and creating.

As a result we experience repeated demotivating thoughts as the Damager circulates its stories of our past "failures" in our minds. While false, the engage us by seeming to be credible and so convincing that we soon find ourselves in an internal court room in which we simultaneously play the parts of victim, defendant and judge.

The mind thus becomes ruminative, and negative thoughts and stories keep repeating. As mentioned earlier, the brain is unable to differentiate between true and false, and thus accepts every thought and feeling as true. We therefore believe our false thoughts, react to their seeming reality, and accordingly define our lives.

In doing so, we create more distortions in our perceptions, thoughts and emotions, and adversely impact our brains.

A good question to ask ourselves, when the Damager plants *not... enough* stories in our minds, is "compared to whom or what?" This reality-based probe unravels the Damager's fallacies, and our having unconsciously agreed with them.

We can unravel the Damager by questioning its premise.

The Damager's Tale

We constantly think about and interpret what happens to us and around us to determine our next steps. We learn about our thoughts and emotions through an internal voice that tells us what our perceptions mean, and how they impact us. We call this inner voice *self-talk*. Most self-talk consists of negative stories because our brain, primarily interested in our physical and emotional safety, continually pumps survival-related information into our minds. In scientific terms, this is called Automatic negative Self-Talk.

Negative self-talk shows up involuntarily, seemingly from nowhere, and disappears again. This is the transitory nature of the mind, in which thoughts appear and just as quickly disappear. But in the meantime, they leave their lasting and damaging impressions on our minds and bodies as they pass through.

Negative self-talk is like a runaway train. As the mind repeats these stories again and again, they take on the illusion of truth, and we come to internalize and believe them.

How to Uncover the Damager

The Damager's negative self-talk and stories share common traits. Learning about them helps interrupt their harmful influence.

Here are their primary characteristics. They are:

- Automatic and appear without our invitation
- Based on a few isolated facts
- Stubborn and repetitive
- Inherently pessimistic
- Believable
- Useless
- Depressing

In brief, the stories we tell ourselves create our inner experience, color our perceptions, determine our thoughts, and poorly impact our being, doing and creating.

How to Quiet the Damager

First, we need to become aware of our negative self-talk.

This can be tricky because it goes on so automatically that we might not even be aware of it. An effective way to become aware of our self-talk is noticing how we feel. If *down* and *demotivated*, the Damager's voice is probably speaking in our mind's background.

Using this awareness, along with the tools we have learned, helps us to quiet the Damager's voice.

Reminder: to get the greatest benefit from the practices, write them down rather than just thinking about them. Writing allows the mind to absorb them more effectively, turning them into experience, and then skill.

The following practices will help you build skills to recognize and quiet the Damager.

Practice

Write three negative stories you tell about yourself. Select the three that come up often and distress you the most. Be brief and very specific.

1. _____

2. _____

3. _____

After you are done, think about how each story may be caused by one or more of the following:

1. Your belief about not being good, capable, or loveable enough.

2. A rule which has not been met. For example:

   - My story is: I am not good enough because my partner/boss/child/friend does not believe in me.

   - My unmet rule is: I "should" be a better partner to get approval.

What have you learned from doing this exercise? Be specific.

_____

_____

How can you use this learning in your daily life? Be specific.

_____

_____

Daily Practice

As you go about your day, pay close attention to the Damager's clues. Be vigilant.

The small mind will justify our false negative thoughts and stories by making them so believable that they seem normal. This is the way it works to maintain its power over us.

Rumi beautifully describes the Damager in saying:
"The fault is in the blamer.
Spirit sees nothing to criticize."

In the next chapter, we will discuss the last negative mind-character, the Fixer, which works very closely with the Damager. You will learn how to recognize it and quiet it as well.

"Just as a snake sheds its skin, we must shed our past over and over again.

~ Buddha

Fourteen
The Fixer

The fourth negative mind-character, after the Reacter, Ruler and Damager, is the Fixer. This character comes alive when we believe the Damager's false stories about not being enough in one way or another. The Fixer promises to pull us out of the downward cycle created by the Damager, and make us feel better.

This alluring offer motivates us to happily oblige. The Fixer has a condition though: we *must* follow its instructions to regain happiness and balance.

But you will soon see that in following the Fixer's demands, we inevitably reactivate the Damager, which sets off a harmful interplay between them. This further deepens and prolongs our stress, strips our inner strength, and makes us even unhappier.

The Fixer and the Damager, more than the other mind-characters, have a special covert connection: **one pulls us down; the other promises to pull us up.**

We get caught in this false cycle, and constantly enable one and then the other, which keeps them both active at our expense.

The Fixer-Damager-Fixer Cycle

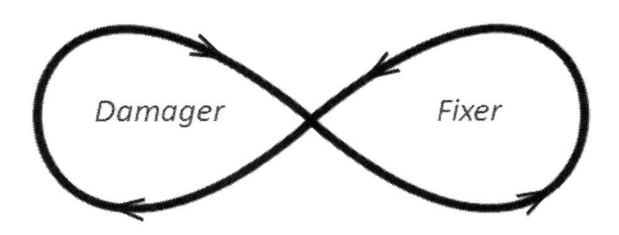

The Fixer in Action

The Fixer, like the Damager, uses stories to get our attention and agreement. However, while the Damager spins negative self-talk that makes us feel down and depressed, the fixer spins a different kind of self-talk which we experience as burst of upbeat energy. This energetic upswing then motivates us to believe the Fixer's stories that we are helping ourselves feel better and accomplish something important. Thus we follow its advice.

This energy creates a sense of urgency and pressure to act quickly. The mind becomes reactive, in turn impairing good judgment, and bypassing the rational thinking. All for negative mind-characters are now in play.

The Fixer's method is to prescribe upbeat and convincing regimens for improvement, such as:

- Be perfect
- Try harder
- Be stronger
- Impress others
- Be smarter
- Be more
- Help others change, be better, stronger and smarter
- Be in more control
- Do more

The Fixer demands perfection. But we will never hit that target because never is never enough.

If you've ever worked for a perfectionist or been in a relationship with one, you know that enough is never enough, standards are arbitrary and constantly changing, and there is no winning regardless of how hard you try. The same principle applies when we want ourselves to be perfect.

The Fixer-Damager Cycle

This is how the close partnership between the Fixer and Damager works. *The Damager creates the illusion that we are damaged, and the Fixer races in with advice on how to improve the illusory damaged self.*

When I want to become better than the way I see myself as being now, it's because the Damager has me convinced that "I am not good enough." When I suddenly feel lonely or disconnected, it's because the Damager has me believe "I am not loveable enough," to which Fixer is responding: "I can help you be that person."

Every one of the Fixer's strategies can be traced to a false thought we have internalized thanks to the Damager.

But those strategies are bound to fail since the notion of being damaged, as real as it may seem at the time, is only an illusion the Damager has created. The Fixer is trying to fix something that is *not* broken or damaged to begin with. By believing and following the Fixer's advice, we will inevitably create damage that does not exist.

When we follow the Fixer's advice, we inevitably create damage that did not exist before.

How to Unravel the Fixer

The way to unravel the Fixer is to understand its game. This is how it plays out:

- First, the Damager traps us into thinking and believing that we are broken or damaged.
- Second, the Fixer convinces us that we need fixing *now,* and spins motivating self-talk containing such phrases as "I need to, I have to, I must," or "I should."
- Third, it convinces us that we would really be helping ourselves by following its instructions.

This entire process creates a rising sense of pressure and restlessness to immediately act.

The Fixer Methods

Thoughts and feelings of not being enough in one way or another, even if illusory, produce emotional pain. Acting on the Fixer's regimens is our way of coping with that pain and restoring our inner balance. But again, in doing so we actually reinforce that pain because we are *trying to fix an illusion – something that does not exist.*

But what are Fixer's methods? Not surprisingly, *they are the mirror opposite of what the Damager has us believe.*

The Fixer's methods are the mirror opposite of the Damager's stories we have believed.

For example, if I hold the thought that I'm not kind or loveable enough, the Fixer instructs me to act more kindly, so I can convince myself and others that I am really a kind and therefore loveable person.

In general, we will involuntarily do everything possible to prove that we are anything but what we have falsely believed about ourselves created by the Damager.

Of course, there is nothing wrong with being kind or going out of our way to help others, and when we are not being driven by the Fixer, these can be a tool for growth and compassion in much more functional ways.

How to Quite the Fixer

Let's move directly into the practices, since by now you have enough background in the workings of the Fixer.

Practice

Write three negative stories you tell about yourself. Select the three which come up often and distress you the most. Be very specific.

Example: "I am incapable of having a good relationship. I am not a nice person. I don't fit. I don't look that good. My background gets in my way of success."

1. _____
2. _____
3. _____

Next, for *each story*, write a specific description of your ideas about how you want to fix yourself.

Example: "I must read relationship books and take a class or two. That should help me to learn how to be a better partner."

1. _____
2. _____
3. _____

Next, notice whether your Ruler is behind why you want to fix yourself. Is there an "I must" or "I should" in your answers above, even if those exact words haven't been used? Write down as many rules as you can find for each story you tell yourself.

My rules are (write as many as you can):

_____   _____
_____   _____
_____   _____
_____   _____
_____   _____

What have you learned in doing this exercise? Be Specific.

_____
_____

How can you use this learning in your daily life? Be specific.

_____

_____

Daily practice

Notice how your Fixer wants to fix you, others and events. Be vigilant toward the signs, such as mental pressure, *body tension* or *feeling driven.*

Step back from reacting. Take a moment to write down the sequence of the negative mind-characters -- Reacter, Ruler, Damager -- that activate the Fixer.

This practice will clearly show you how closely chained these four negative mind-characters really are and how one activates the other, and how this vicious cycle leaves us with emotional scars.

You can break the chain by quieting the negative mind-characters in a timely manner, and saving yourself much unnecessary grief.

Our "fixing" desires feeds the judgments we have against ourselves and others. Those judgments keep the small mind active and make us rigid.

Our judgments express themselves in wanting to fix ourselves and others.

Once we become aware of the Fixer's games and strategies, our desire to "fix" wanes. This leads to the self-acceptance and compassion for ourselves and others that the judgmental mind blocks.

J. Krishnamurti express this well: *"The highest form of human intelligence is to observe yourself without judgment."*

The key is awareness, right understanding and persistence until we overcome the small mind and build the necessary skills to mastering the Self.

It's up to you.

Fifteen

Putting It All Together

In the last four chapters we looked into the specific workings of the small mind and how it uses four negative modes of thinking or characters to make our minds unproductive. We also covered how these four characters enable each other and create a snowball effect which further strengthens their harmful impact, and in turn reshapes the brain in useless ways.

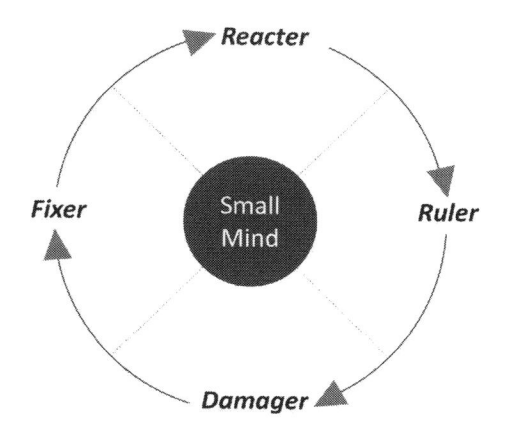

The Small Mind in Sum

We first took apart the small mind to understand how it distorts our thoughts and creates illusions about who we are.

Let's now examine how we experience the small mind in sum.

1. The small mind thrives on constantly *thinking, analyzing, comparing, judging, projecting, fantasizing*, and *making up stories*. It does so even when there's no possible payoff. It feeds on our attention, which takes our focus away from our *senses* and therefore from the awareness of the present. Since our senses are the bridge to our big mind, in bypassing them we become consumed with over-thinking and thus stuck in the small mind.

2. Since the small mind is rooted in fear, the thoughts it generates *won't lead to thinking, understanding or insight* useful *in the real world.* Its useless activities just kick up dirt, keep us in a fog, and create anxiety.

3. Thoughts generated by the small mind have a chaotic quality, and keep repeating themselves. This over-thinking activity becomes habitual and addictive, and unavoidably exhausts our resiliency and vitality.

As a result, our attention becomes erratic, distracting us from present reality, and we end up making decisions that *lead us away* from productive ways of being, doing and creating.

What the Small Mind Demands

The small mind and its four characters want constant:

- Attention
- Acceptance
- Affection
- Appreciation
- Authority

Each of these demands keeps alive the Reacter, the Ruler, the Damager and the Fixer. For instance when we seek attention, we are feeding the Damager's story about not being worthy. When we seek authority we are feeding the Ruler's demand for control.

The more we try to meet any of the small mind's five demands listed above, the more the negative mind-characters adversely impact our lives.

The small mind has a crafty way of keeping itself active. When it *gets what it wants*, it is happy, and naturally wants more. It therefore *calls up one of the negative mind-characters to get more of it*. Thus we behave in ways to get even more attention, acceptance, affection, appreciation and authority.

On the other hand, the small mind becomes annoyed and reactive when it *does not get* what it wants. It then *prompts the four mind-characters into action to assure it will get what it wants.*

As we can see, whether it's happy or unhappy, the small mind causes us emotional pain, distress and anxiety. In reality, by acting on the small mind's commands, we end up creating even more tension and imbalance throughout our minds and bodies.

Whichever way we try to please the small mind, it causes us emotional pain.

What we need most is to heal the emotional pain the small mind creates.

Let's be clear that there is absolutely nothing wrong in wanting attention, acceptance, affection, appreciation or authority. *Those natural desires become harmful only when they originate from the distorted thoughts and stories that the small mind and its four characters circulate in our minds.*

The trick is to rapidly recognize the small mind's illusions and interrupt the distorted thinking we create by believing them.

Chaining and Snowballing

Let's take a look at an actual example of how the four negative mind-characters' chaining together and snowballing impact our lives. While this may not represent your own current life, our brains and minds all work in pretty much the same way.

Joanna (not her actual name), a woman in her early fifties, came up to me after I had finished a talk, asking me whether taking my workshop would be of help to her relationship. In return I asked, "What kind of help does your relationship need?"

"He (her partner) doesn't seem to care anymore, and I cannot change that, no matter what I do," she sighed.

"Does he want to be changed?" I asked.

"I am not sure if he can. He is so set in his ways, he does not even listen to my suggestions anymore," she responded.

"Can you share with me one of your suggestions?" I nudged.

"Well, like...he should finish his degree; like....he should become more active, spend more time with me. Nothing big;

small stuff like that. Do you think taking your workshop will help?" she continued.

In my usual response, I said "*it's really up to you.*"

I now had a good inkling about what might be lurking beneath! I wanted her to come to that decision herself, because the path of Self-mastery works by taking responsibility.

I was somewhat surprised to see Joanna sitting in the second row of my next workshop. As we went through unpeeling the covers of the inner working of the small mind through discussions and exercises, she had increasing "Aha" moments. The following is an account of her sharing in the group, which I have pieced together.

In the process of exploring her mind, Joanna came to understand how she had been trying to *fix* her husband – he *should* do this or that – all under the disguise of "I care about our relationship." To her surprise, the more she tried, the more uncaring he became! Her attempts to help him so that the relationship could be helped was based on her opinion that he had more potential than he thought himself. ("He is not good enough" silently echoed by her Damager). That was why she had been trying to motivate him to do something about that (her Ruler in action).

Joanna would get upset (her Reacter) whenever they discussed the subject. He would just say "of course, dear" and continue being who he was. ("Not capable enough" reinforced by her Damager.) Not only were her attempts at *fixing* not working, they actually made the relationship even more tense (her Damager-Fixer-Damager cycle). Naturally they became even more isolated from one another, and their relationship suffered even more.

Joanna left the workshop with a new understanding of how her perceptions, emotions and behaviors have been the source of her own struggles, and how they naturally spill over to the closest person in her life.

I saw Joanna a few months later at a gathering. She was glowing while introducing her partner Randall to me. I really wanted to know how things were going, especially since I noticed they are holding hands and looking at each other tenderly often. But I did not want to pry.

She must have sensed my curiosity and offered: "Oh, I shared everything with Randall," she said. "I stopped fixing him and all the other things you said in the class: the Damager, Ruler and all that…they just disappeared. I am not saying they don't show up at times. But I know how to quiet them now. My mind now lets me enjoy the real Randall much more."

"The strange thing is," she continued, "my relationships with my boss, parents and friends have also become a lot more enjoyable!"

I then asked Randall how things are with him. "It has been so much better," he said. "I have actually started doing some of the things we had talked about since I don't feel pushed and unappreciated anymore."

I thanked Joanna for being there for herself and said this to her and Randall before saying goodbye: *We take ourselves with us wherever we go.*

As I mentioned earlier, Joanna's situation might be different from yours. However, because we share a standard brain, the human mind, excepting subtle cultural nuances, functions much the same way.

The Small Mind Effect in Sum

Having looked at how the small mind's characters work, let's now consider their sum effect on us.

The small mind, persistent in wanting *attention, acceptance, affection, appreciation and authority* will do anything to get it regardless of how it impacts us. In this pursuit, the small mind convinces us that our survival is in danger, poses as our protector, and takes control of our minds.

The small mind has one end goal: convincing us to think, feel and ultimately believe that we are powerless without it. Period

Having personal power, in my view, means one thing: *the ability to intentionally lead our minds, and in turn our lives, in a productive way, one that benefits us and others*. This is true power and the foundation of inner freedom and happiness.

Powerlessness, on the other hand, leads us to mistake our distorted thoughts for ourselves, and indiscriminately act on them.

Believing that we are powerless impacts us in two crucial ways:

- First, the small mind takes the driver's seat, makes our decisions, and runs our lives on our behalf. The smallest things begin to trigger us. We demand that we, others, and the world in general *should* conform to our rules. When they do not, we make up false stories, believe them, and react.

  To make up for our reactivity, we then try to fix ourselves, others, and conditions as quickly as possible. Since the Fixer and Damager enable one another, *this process keeps gaining momentum, deepening our pain and stealing our vigor.*

- Second, since *beliefs and perceptions go hand-in-hand*, we start perceiving ourselves as victims. We begin to view others as authorities more powerful than ourselves, and external circumstances as the main cause of our challenges in life.

  As a result, we start looking for answers outside of ourselves, and shy away from living life fully, feeling unable to productively steer our lives on our own.

All of these harmful effects are *the direct result of believing thoughts formed by the secretion of droplets of chemicals in the brain, which our untrained minds then distort.*

This is the simple but powerful reality of what we unconsciously allow to happen to us and our lives.

When we learn how to use our minds skillfully, our thoughts become clear and useful, and we once again become masters of our lives.

In Summary

We examined how the four negative mind-characters impact us in adverse ways.

We looked into personal triggers and how learning about them allows us to avoid reacting, but respond instead. We also detailed how these mind-characters are chained and automatically activate one another. And finally we learned how quieting them allows us to sidestep the small mind, and connect with our big mind to lead productive and happy lives.

The reason we talked about all four negative mind-characters instead of just focusing on the one, which starts the whole harmful chain of events, is that we are not always able to recognize our triggers quickly enough to prevent becoming reactive.

Second, most of us have lived with the three other mind-characters throughout our entire lives.

Therefore, learning to recognize each of the four mind-characters is essential to disrupting the small mind's routine, regardless of which begins the cycle.

In the next chapter we will learn more methods for quieting the small mind so we can skillfully use our thoughts to master the Self.

Sixteen

The Grand Paradox

Understanding the concept of paradox will help us better recognize the facets of human nature, and how they influence the process of mastering the Self.

What is a paradox? A paradox combines features or qualities that *seem* to be in opposition while conveying a single meaning. Here are a few simple examples of paradoxes:

- Bittersweet
- The beginning of the end
- Deep down, he is really shallow
- The wise fool
- And the famous one by Socrates: "I know one thing -- that I know nothing."

As we can see, these phrases combine contradictory qualities while conveying a unified idea. This is the nature of the paradox.

The experience of life can be understood as a paradox as well.

We have paradoxical relationships with many parts of our lives, beginning with the way our brains function and extending to the physical laws that govern the world.

Let's start with our brain, the director of our being.

On one hand, it constantly seeks balance, while forcing itself out of balance by continually collecting volumes of negative information that agitate it.

The imbalance the brain creates then forces the small mind and the big mind to oppose one another, which brings chaos and reactivity to our minds, bodies and lives.

Next: from the first days of our lives our brains strongly favor safety and oppose change.

Thus we constantly pursue stability and consistency in every aspect of our lives, although the reality is that change and impermanence are the only constants in the world.

So we relentlessly pursue that which realistically does not, and cannot exist.

Next: we split our self-unity by wanting only the *good*, and resisting whatever we consider *bad*. We don't seem to realize that the bad – our dark side, our shadow and our unwanted consequences – our inseparable from us.

So we try to achieve unity by separating ourselves.

In general, we unconsciously resist life's inherent changeability, impermanence and uncontrollability, while desperately seeking to live balanced lives.

This paradoxical approach to life lies at the center of our ineffectiveness and unhappiness.

In adopting this good/bad, right/wrong and black/white outlook, we create forces within us which return to us the very same thing we are resisting.

But the negative mind-characters will not disappear by resisting or ignoring them. They will lurk in the background, quietly *defeating our ways of being, doing and creating*.

That is why they are named the dark side or shadow – they remain in the background as the unwanted and unrecognized aspects of ourselves.

When we fail to recognize or accept our dark sides, we notice them in others. For example, someone says or does something which triggers us, we see it as *their* flaw, but only because we share the same characteristic and fail to recognize it in ourselves. How else would we know?

Thus by being unaware of our shadow sides we create *blind spots* for ourselves.

"*I am not who you think I am. You are what you think I am,*" a quote that elegantly describes the notion of blind spots we develop about ourselves.

Blind spots rattle the small mind in subtle ways, and open the path for it to tap into our thoughts, distort them and create illusions. Stress sets in, reactivity replaces objectivity and we unconsciously act on our impulses and illusions.

Unintentionally we create emotional pain, and since pain is unwelcome, we resist it. This forces the brain and then the mind further out of balance, and widens the gap between how we perceive our *light* and *dark* sides.

We cannot, therefore, simply focus on and want only the bright side. That is only one part of who we are.

As Carl Jung put it: *"One does not become enlightened by imagining figures of light, but by making the darkness conscious."*

To restore balance, we spend a great deal of time and energy negotiating between these *seemingly* opposing poles, not realizing that the *light* and the *dark* are complementary, rather than opposing; that one cannot exist without the other, as day cannot exist without the night.

We seem to forget that we can see our goodness because our shadow makes it stand out. Without our shadow we cannot distinguish our light.

Together, once we accept them all as an undeniable parts of ourselves, they can form the finest aspects of our characters.

True mastery begins to emerge from this acceptance.

In realizing this, our unity and that of others come into focus. We can then use the significant time and energy we save in *not resisting* to lead far more fulfilling and productive lives.

This is the process of accepting, or what I call *befriending* which we will explore in the next chapter.

Here is a practice to help you recognize your paradoxical views.

Practice

Select three people in your life who have characteristics you dislike. Make a brief, specific list of what about them bothers you. Note everything that comes to mind, without filtering or rationalizing your thoughts.

Person 1: _____

What I don't like about:

_____
_____
_____

Person 2: _____

What I don't like about:

_____
_____
_____

Person 3: _____

What I don't like about:

_____
_____
_____

When you are done, go through your list and take out any repeats. For example, if you dislike the same thing about two different people, just pick it once. Then list the top five things you dislike about them below.

1. _____
2. _____
3. _____
4. _____
5. _____

This list most probably represents your own unrecognized shadows, which you notice in others. Adopt one of those for a day, and accept it as your own. You will soon notice that what you dislike about "them" no longer triggers you.

As Carl Jung noted: *"Everything that irritates us about another can lead us to understanding ourselves."*

The *understanding* he is referring to is in accepting the inherently paradoxical nature of life, which will transform our darkness into brightness, energizing us toward mastering the Self.

Our brightness reveals itself when we direct our thoughts from resisting that which we *think* of as our darkness toward befriending it.

The Self is the combination of our bright and dark sides. We can only master it when we resolve that paradox by accepting that we are simultaneously both.

I have saved the grandest paradox for last:

The Self or the big mind resides within the small mind.

But this would be like saying that a big ball fits inside a much smaller ball. It logically just doesn't make sense. But it does in this case.

Why this paradox?

Because the small mind meets our survival needs by acting as our "protector." We need the small mind for that purpose, but we do not need its four negative characters which, when acting unruly, block the way to our Self.

We must therefore bring the four mind-characters under our direction by *befriending* them, which quiets the small mind's fearful nature while maintaining its useful functions.

The Self or the big mind is right around that corner. There is no short cut; this *is* the short cut to mastering the Self.

It's really up to you.

Seventeen

Let's Be Friends

In past chapters I have used the term *quieting* to describe a method for reducing the small mind's activities and returning it to its calm natural state.

Let's explore it here more deeply.

Befriending means that we see things as they realistically are, **without wanting to change or fix them**, including our own self, others, and events.

It means accepting reality, adapting to it and using it to produce what we want.

When we acknowledge that we all have Reacters, Rulers, Damagers and Fixers, and accept that they can serve useful purposes, we are befriending them.

For example, I do want my Reacter to push me out of the way when a car is fast approaching. I do want my Ruler to reign me in when one more drink will cause me to drive dangerously. I do want my Damager to remind me, in a helpful way how to use past challenges to create better results. And finally, I do want my Fixer to help me improve my skills in areas in which I can become more productive.

When we befriend our negative mind-characters, we are no longer resisting them. This quiets down their negative aspects, and allows them to serve us in beneficial ways.

As you recall, we enable the small mind by either entertaining or resisting our thoughts. We resist our thoughts when we feel vulnerable.

But how do we entertain them?

We entertain our thoughts in two ways. First, we **analyze and attach meaning** to them. Second, we try to **change them**. In either case, we breed new life into them.

For instance, analyzing requires that we compare one thing to another so we can reach a conclusion. In doing so, we routinely attach meanings to those thoughts: *good, bad, right* and *wrong*, and set out to find their deeper messages and meanings.

Let's say we experience a thought: *I am not ... enough,* which is the Damager talking. We then entertain that thought by asking ourselves why, where it came from, what I may have done to bring it up, and what I should do differently to be *good enough* again.

We then dwell on those after thoughts, obsess over them, and reach conclusions about the past and future. We have now invited the Damager to enter our mind's stage.

The second way we entertain our thoughts is by trying to change our negative ones to positive ones, believing negative thoughts to be *bad* and positive ones *good*. In doing so, the value we have attached to this new thought – *good* – openly invites the Fixer, energizing it and getting it involved.

One popular method for motivating ourselves in such situations is to use positive affirmations. We tell ourselves *"I am strong, I am a good person, I can do this."*

We have now started the Damager-Fixer-Damager cycle.

Let's explore how.

If I truly felt that I am a strong person, a good person, or can do anything I wish to, would I need to convince myself through affirmations?

After all, when we use affirmations to change our thoughts or behavior, it is generally because we are *holding the opposite deep within us.* In other words, we have already bought into the Damager's premise that we are *not ... enough*, which leads us to follow the Fixer's advice as how to repair that damage through a positive affirmation.

Any Fixer activity, as you'll recall, will initially feel energizing and seem like a step in the right direction. The brain, however, which constantly produces negative information – which continues until we die and the brain stops working – interprets things differently.

So when the Damager spreads negative stories about us, and the Fixer steps in to reverse them, the push and pull between the two creates resistance, which alarms the brain.

The alarmed brain responds by more strongly reinforcing our original negative thoughts about *not being... enough,* the Fixer then more strongly persuades us to fix ourselves as quickly as possible. The push/pull gets stronger and we fall into the Damager-Fixer-Damager cycle.

In short, we try to put out the fire by throwing gasoline on it.

We become like Hollywood movie producers directing the actions of our mental activities. As we get drawn in to more and more negative stories, we become more emotionally convinced that we are damaged and need fixing. This sets off more reactions, the mind becomes more agitated and the brain grows increasingly unbalanced.

The small mind, off course, enjoys this process of being invited into and taking part in our mental movies, as this sustains its energy.

It is wise to avoid the small mind cycle altogether. Zen master Shunryu Suzuki *says it elegantly: "Leave your front door and your back door open. Allow your thoughts to come and go. Just don't serve them tea."*

How do we let our thoughts come and go without getting attached to them by either entertaining or resisting them?

By befriending them.

How Befriending Works

Befriending is a method for allowing thoughts to remain in their native state; passing through our minds like the wind passing down streets without clinging to every wall, door and window.

When we use befriending, we let things unfold without attaching *good, bad, right* or *wrong* to them.

This applies to befriending even our distorted thoughts: when we experience *I am not ... enough*, we just notice that thought *without reacting, liking, believing, resisting or ignoring it*. We just consider it just a thought *without any inherent meaning*. And this is right, since the *only* meanings thoughts have are those that we attach to them.

We intervene and energize our distorted thoughts by resisting, reacting, ignoring, liking, or believing them.

When we do not intervene, the mind returns to its calm natural state, and resistance, which keeps the negative mind-characters engaged, automatically dissolves.

What is Resistance?

Most of us, enabled by our survival instincts believe that *resisting* – a subtle form of fighting – safeguards us from physical and emotional vulnerability. This is far from fact.

Let's more deeply explore the notion of resistance since it plays an influential role on the workings of the brain and mind.

Whenever we face conditions we view as undesirable – potential threats to our physical or emotional well-being, or thoughts or emotions we don't like – we *push back* or *resist* as a way to ensure our safety.

Resistance naturally generates stress. The word stress refers to our physical and emotional response to a demand that forces us out of our comfort zone. These responses can sometimes help, providing bursts of energy to escape danger, but it is when such responses are a reaction to something emotional that we begin to suffer.

Stress is also one of the biggest factors determining the levels of serotonin in the brain. Serotonin is a brain chemical messenger which transmits nerve impulses between nerve cells or neurons, and plays an important part in regulating our mood, learning, motivation and sleep.

We resist in different ways depending on the situation. For instance, when we have thoughts that make us feel bad, we resist them by trying to ignore them, argue against them or distract ourselves, hoping to calm our minds.

We also resist whenever we try to do anything that is different than what we have done in the past, or different from what conditions exist now.

But *resistance actually creates the opposite of what we hope for* because it inevitably re-energizes the anxiety-producing thoughts, deepens our stress, and makes the mind even more unsettled.

Resistance, while we view it as undesirable, *is what we naturally do whenever we move in any direction.* When, for example we drive, we create drag or resistance against the car's body by pushing it through the air. When we walk, we create resistance against our bodies by stirring the air around us. When we talk, we create resistance by pushing the air.

In the same way, when we try move ourselves in a new direction – as you may be by reading this book and doing the practices – we create natural resistance and tension throughout our systems. The brain, ever seeking balance, resists our efforts by creating fear in the hopes of dissuading us and returning us to the comfort zone of *what was*.

Thus resistance, as it relates to personal development, is by its very nature self-sabotaging because it *unconsciously* blocks us from learning, developing and growing.

Dissolving Resistance

Resistance, for most of us, has become second nature. The small mind and its four characters expect it and often produce it to energize themselves.

Resistance feeds on itself. As long as it receives yet more resistance, it thrives. But it does not expect to be approached differently, such as by being befriended which it cannot defend itself against. Thus *befriending naturally discharges the energy of resistance* and *dissolves stress*.

We become hard and rigid when we resist. We become flexible and compassionate when we befriend resistance.

In one of the previous chapters we witnessed Joanna recognizing how she sabotaged her relationship. But once she learned how to befriend her negative mind-characters, they lost their influence on her and became allies, helping her to establish constructive relationships all around.

When we dissolve the energy of resistance by intentionally befriending it, we unlock our potential, and discover far more productive ways of being, doing and creating.

Recognizing Resistance

Again, the most effective way to recognize resistance is to notice when we feel tension, unease and restlessness in our minds and bodies.

Whenever we notice these effects, the opposite of the calm natural mind, *we are resisting something within or around us.*

Once we learn to recognize resistance, we can consciously sidestep it by using a befriending tool called Thought Labeling to return the mind to its calm natural state.

Thought Labeling Tool

Thought labeling is an effective mind training tool for quieting the mind's resistance and befriending our thoughts. By labeling our thoughts we acknowledge them, and then let them go on their way without having them play on our mind's stage.

We start using this tool by first training the mind to recognize whether a given thought is *useful* or not, how to pick the *useful* ones, and let go of the others.

Productive thinking flows from this selection process.

Over time, we will come to realize the fact that *we are not our thoughts. This is one of the most fundamental and important of all realizations at the core of mastering the Self.*

Thought labeling has been used for hundreds of years in contemplative practices, and has been proven by modern science as an effective tool for redirecting our minds away from unproductive thoughts and restoring attention and balance. [104,105,106,107]

How Thought Labeling Works

We start by acknowledging a thought and *intentionally refraining* from reacting, attaching any meaning, analysis, or assumption to it.

This *interrupts the thought's flow* before it has the chance to lodge in our minds, activate the negative mind-characters, and leave unhelpful impressions on the brain.

The Benefits of Thought Labeling

This tool beneficially impacts the brain by interrupting its ineffective patterns, and making new neural pathways and connections. This also usefully influences the mind.

When you practice thought labeling you become skillful at *shifting your mind from looking from your thoughts to looking at your thoughts.*

When you *look* at your thoughts, you can decide objectively whether a thought is useful, or let it go. **The nature of a thought changes when you observe it rather than act on it.**

Thought labeling is simple tool, and gets easier and more effective with practice. Two important facts about thought labeling: first, it is an *on-the-go* tool we can quietly use anytime and anywhere; second, it works most effectively when we use it in the *heat of the moment* – as soon as we notice a *useless* thought arising in our minds.

In short, thought labeling offers these benefits:

- It increases our awareness of our thoughts and emotions, thus putting us in charge of transforming our habitual negative thinking patterns.
- It creates a gap between us and our thoughts, allowing us to easily recognize our reactions, and step back from them. This prevents our stress-response system from releasing harmful hormones in our minds and bodies.
- Absent those harmful hormones, our minds stop spinning negative narratives, freeing us to access our higher-order thinking abilities. We gain objectivity and resiliency.
- With greater resiliency, we bring the mind under our conscious direction. This will restore the mind and brain to their calm natural states.
- With a calm mind, we will experience increasing freedom and power in our being, doing and creating.

This is Self-mastery or self-directed neuroplasticity in action -- with you in charge of it.

Step-by-Step

We simply label any thought that produces agitation, judgment, confusion, unease, self-doubt, or insecurity in our minds and bodies as **useless.**

We will then be left with thoughts that are useful and productive.

We label thoughts by using the "triple A" steps below:

1. **Acknowledging**: Notice that a thought has shown up, and whether it is producing unease in your mind or body.

2. **Accepting**: If it is, avoid resisting, rejecting or attaching *good, bad, right* or *wrong* to it. Also refrain from naming it; for example, if you are angry, don't label that thought or emotion *anger.* Use a meaningless word if you have to.

   Just stand by and notice the thought coming and going in your mind, and let it simply pass without attachment or naming.

3. **Applying**: Label that thought *useless* and move on without investigating the thought or the emotion further.

Example: I'm driving on the freeway when a car cuts me off. I feel tightness in my jaw and in my grip on the wheel. My mind begins to race, and I notice an urge to teach the other driver a lesson by doing the same.

This is a *heat of the moment* opportunity to label that thought *useless* and prevent triggering. This allows us to continue on our way without causing internal agitation or an incident.

Becoming skillful at thought labeling requires practice. But when we do, it becomes an energy that can move mountains.

In sum, the "triple A" steps in action are:

Acknowledge it + Accept it unconditionally + Label it ***useless*** + move on = Free yourself from the useless thinking -> productive thoughts and emotions.

Practice

Whenever a thought or emotion produces tension, shutdown, judgment or chaos, label it *useless*.

Example:

<u>Traffic is *horrible*</u>	<u>I feel *tense*</u>	***<u>Useless</u>***
Thought	Emotion	Label

Think of four thoughts that cause you stress, anger or unhappiness. Example: My work is stressing me. I cannot do this. I should look better. I am not appreciated.

Write down them in triple A steps, reciting each to yourself in your inner voice.

Thought	Emotion	Label
_____	_____	_____
Thought	Emotion	Label
_____	_____	_____
Thought	Emotion	Label
_____	_____	_____
Thought	Emotion	Label

Practice 1

Think of three thoughts you experience when you are feeling down or when you make a mistake you feel you should not have.

Write down them in triple A steps, reciting each to yourself in your inner voice.

Thought	Emotion	Label
Thought	Emotion	Label
Thought	Emotion	Label

Some Helpful Tips:

If, after using the Triple A steps in the *heat of the moment*, you still find yourself dwelling on the thought or emotion, notice whether related thoughts or emotions are crossing your mind. If so, label them *useless* as well. *Move on without thinking about them any longer.*

Notice the quality of your thoughts and emotions after one week's practice.

Use any occasion available to you to practice. Our jobs, families, environments, and how we feel about ourselves all offer plenty of daily opportunities.

Once we learn to neutralize our useless thoughts by mastering thought labeling, we have begun to befriend our thoughts and started to transform them from distorted into productive states.

This is developing and growing ourselves versus improving and changing ourselves.

Through this training, the mind becomes more objective, more alert and more productive.

Earlier in the book we discussed how our thoughts are central to shaping our ways of being, doing and creating. And how they offer us *single point of focus* through which we can develop and grow all three at once. *Choosing useful thoughts offers the tool.*

Self-mastery is the process of creating a cohesive and productive life experience that begins with how skillfully we handle our thoughts.

"Watch your thoughts, they become words;
watch your words, they become actions;
watch your actions, they become habits;
watch your habits, they become character;
watch your character, for it becomes your destiny."

~ Lao Tzu

Eighteen

Out of My Way Please

This book's premise is that we can master the Self by overcoming the mind's limiting forces which become obstacles separating us from it.

We explored those obstacles by peeling away the small mind to expose its four negative characters which produce our distorted thoughts.

Those characters often hide in our blind spots, make themselves difficult to recognize, while setting off additional damaging modes of thinking which also hide in the same places.

Let's explore the concept of blind spots since they act as a shield for the those mind-characters..

When driving a car, blind spots are areas of the road we can't see either in looking straight ahead or in our mirrors.

Just as we experience blind spots when driving, we also have mental blind spots – aspects of our character and behavior hidden from our conscious view.

How can we learn to identify our blind spots? ***A reactive mind and ensuing behavior is a reliable indication.***

Why? Because you'll recall, the Reacter is the first noticeable of the four mind-characters to engage which then activates the other three. It's only after they expand beyond our blind spots that we become aware of the tension and unease they have creates in our minds and bodies.

This is why we explored each of the mind-characters separately and in detail. This will allow us to more easily move them from our blind spots to our bright spots – conscious awareness – and in time eliminate their impact.

Why is this important? Carl Jung aptly clarifies the point: "until you make the unconscious conscious, it will direct your life and you will call it fate."

Once the four negative mind-characters become habitual thinking modes, aside from their own harmful influence, they produce other damaging modes of thinking. These modes also operate from within our blind spots, and block our way to mastering the Self.

I invite you to pay special attention to those that may ring true for you. Write *a brief description of how they show up in your life in your note book.* This awareness will help you sidestep their influence.

Before we start, let's review Chapter 2's definition of right understanding: *It's when we have a direct experience without interference or distortion, and as they actually are.*

On the flip side of right understanding is *misunderstanding: It's when interference from our distorted thoughts mislead our perceptions and thoughts.*

Let's explore some of the key thought distortions that mislead our minds:

1. **I Am My Thoughts**. The first misunderstanding is mistaking the *stream of thoughts* constantly passing through our minds *for who we are.*

    By falsely identifying with our thoughts we allow them to control our emotions and behavior.

    Furthermore, when we identify with our distorted thoughts, we unconsciously identify with the problems they create, and inevitably become those problems.

    We then constantly look for problems – *what is or could be wrong* in ourselves, others and our surroundings – we push the mind more deeply into reactivity, and unconsciously look for even more that's wrong.

    We can sidestep this obstacle, the illusion that 'I am my thoughts,' by regularly using the thought labeling tool to step out of those distortions.

2. **Stress or Failure**. The second misunderstanding is to label a sense of pressure or tension as failure.

    Whenever we try *anything* new, from taking a walk in a new neighborhood to trying unfamiliar food, we produce some degree of tension throughout our systems. This is natural for the brain when it hasn't yet created neural pathways to handle unfamiliar experiences.

After all, *tension is a natural driving force needed for nearly any change we attempt to achieve*. Let's use an experiment to demonstrate. Please read the short instructions first.

Pick up a rubber band, put it the palm of one hand, and observe how in this *relaxed* state the band is free of tension.

Now hold one end of the rubber band with two fingers, and stretch it by pulling the band outward with two fingers of your other hand. In doing so, you are creating tension in the band's structure.

Holding the band away from your face, let go of one of the ends. This will make the band leap through the air in either a forward or backward direction.

Thus stretching and stressing the formerly resting rubber provides the *propelling force* without which it would have remained in the same position.

Now go back and do the exercise.

The same principle applies to us. When we want to develop ourselves beyond where we are now, we unconsciously stretch ourselves. This challenges our existing thoughts, especially the distorted ones, and disturbs our comfort zones.

In doing so we are creating internal tension needed as a propelling force.

This is key: *when the calm natural mind inspires us to stretch ourselves, we propel ourselves forward. But when* *distorted thoughts push us to stretch, we experience tension, anxiety and propel ourselves backwards.*

What leads us to view tension as either limiting or advancing is the source of our thoughts – whether they are from the small mind or the big mind.

When our thoughts lead us to view tension as limiting, we try to lower it by telling ourselves *Fixer* stories: "*it's ok, look at the positive side, go shopping, have a drink, watch TV, tomorrow will be a brighter day,*" and other dismissive slogans.

But by trying to fix the natural tension arising from our desire to grow, we essentially create an opposing force which undermines our efforts.

Natural tension is needed as propelling energy. We create opposing forces and undermine our efforts when we try to artificially reduce it. All we need to do is to change how we view and interpret stress.

According to research from the Hardiness Research Lab at University of California Irvine, "*Those who view stress as inevitable in life events thrive. People who thrive, instead of trying to avoid stress, look for effective ways to engage with it, adapt to it, and learn from it.*"

Multiple studies show that by consciously bringing our stress-response under control lowers the level of stress hormones we release in our bodies.

Thus we can experience stress, rather than as paralyzing, as force for thriving. [102,103,104]

We can sidestep the obstacle of 'tension as failure' by befriending the small mind, which effortlessly taps us into the big mind, allowing us to adapt and use tension as a constructive propelling force.

3. **Demonizing the Ego.** The third misunderstanding is about the role ego plays in our lives.

There is much demonizing of the ego, in both modern and ancient teachings, as the elusive evil behind many of the bad things we do, and how it ultimately blocks our happiness, progress and enlightenment.

Much advice is also given about denying, ignoring, disowning or outright killing of the ego as the most worthwhile undertaking if we want to master ourselves and lead truly happy lives.

In 2014, for instance, I attended a gathering where the presenter spoke at length about the ills of the ego. "*Do yourselves the favor of your lifetime by destroying this ruthless character,*" he passionately implored. The audience, nodding their heads, seemed to agree.

I made my way toward him afterwards and earnestly asked if he could help me understand where to find my ego. After all, I needed to locate my ego to "destroy" it.

"What do you mean?" he asked, surprised. *"It's all over. It runs your life. It's perhaps the one who has put you up to ask this question."*

We chatted for a while more and I went on to ask whether, to fundamentally *do away* with the ego as he proposed, wouldn't it be advisable to first get to know what I'm trying to oust.

He launched into even deeper philosophical explanations, giving me examples as to how "kill" my ego, such as disciplining it to the point of suffocation.

My question remaining unanswered, and I returned to my seat.

Let's explore the notion of the ego from a different perspective.

The word *ego* is often used as a broad term which leads to confusion. And advice regarding its destruction usually involves complex psycho-spiritual analysis that goes above most people's heads -- certainly above mine.

I would like to offer my thoughts in regard to the role of the ego and how it relates to our day-to-day lives, as well as our Self-mastery.

In his model of the psyche Freud defined the Id, ego and super-ego as the three central parts of our mental lives. [108,109,110,111] *Each has abilities which not only support our survival, but also help us function daily.*

The id, connected to our survival instincts, operates [on a] primitive level. It is ruled by the Pleasure Principle [and] combined with its primitive instincts, causes the [id to] *demand* that our bodily needs, wants and des[ires be] fulfilled immediately or it will go into reactive mod[e.]

For example, when a baby is born and until i[t reaches] around the age of five, the id dominates his or her behavior to assure its highest priority: survival.

The id, if not managed properly, runs adults' behavior due to our survival instincts.

The ego, the second part of our psyche, develops later in life and manages the id's primitive desires and often unrealistic demands to make sure that they are appropriate in the real world, and following them will not cause us harm. For example, if my id wants to steal food from the store because I am hungry, or get totally naked in public because it's too hot outside, the ego intervenes and helps me consider the long-term consequences of my actions before acting on them.

As we can see the ego, which is more realistic than the id, comes up with sensible strategies to help us behave in beneficial ways.

But when the *ego loses balance*, it can no longer manage the id's demands. The id therefore leads us to behave in inappropriate or harmful ways to ourselves and others. For example, stealing or getting naked.

The third part of our psyche is the super-ego, which reminds us of cultural rules, what is appropriate and acceptable, and what is not. We learn most of these rules and values from significant others such as our parents, teachers and other authority figures.

The super-ego strives for perfection and wants us to become our ideal selves, and achieve our higher goals in life.

This trio -- id, ego and the super-ego -- interact with each other in interesting ways.

For example, the id and the super-ego often have opposing desires. The id is instinctual and immediate, while the super-ego thinks in the long-term.

The ego therefore takes the position of a mediator between the conflicting wishes of the id and super-ego so we can maintain balance in our daily lives.

As we can see, *the ego*, contrary to its portrayal as the wicked evil enemy, *plays an essential role without which we cannot function properly.*

The ego becomes destructive only when it loses its ability to effectively manage the id. It is therefore critical to determine how the ego loses that ability, and how to restore it.

How does an out of Balance Ego Behave?

The out of balance ego becomes increasingly and unreasonably demanding, and not surprisingly, its acts become similar to that of the small mind: wanting *attention, acceptance, affection, appreciation and authority* at all costs.

The ego, like the overactive small mind, creates turmoil when it doesn't get what it wants, when and how it wants them.

Otherwise, the ego is crucial to mediating between the id and the super-ego. Therefore the advice that it must be destroyed neither serves any useful purpose nor actually works.

As we can see, the claim that the ego in general is inherently bad only applies when it's out of balance.

In fact, if we try to discipline or destroy the ego, we set up a fight within ourselves which sets off nothing but resistance. This is clearly counterproductive, will only push the ego into greater imbalance and dysfunction, and push us further away from mastering the Self.

C.S Lewis perfectly expressed what is wrong with the promise that we will gain humility in exchange for "destroying" the ego: *"True humility is not thinking less of yourself; it is thinking of yourself less."*

In essence, our ego is neither the problem nor responsible for our mishaps and ineffectiveness. Rather, our useless thoughts which distort our emotions and behaviors are to blame.

We can sidestep 'demonizing the ego' by simply noticing when we are *craving* attention, acceptance, affection, appreciation and authority, and choose to consciously bypass behaviors intended to seek them.

An effective way is to pay close attention to which of the four mind-characters -- Reacter, Ruler, Damager or the Fixer -- are causing our craving. Once you identify the culprit, use the tools you have learned to befriend them. This will quickly return the ego to its state of balance helping us to function properly in our daily lives.

4. **Out There**. The fourth crucial misunderstanding is believing that answers are outside of us, and we must search outwardly to find them.

    The main cause of this outlook is lack of self-trust, often beginning when we believe that regardless of what we do, we will repeat our past "failures" in the future.

    We therefore choose the past as a place of residence rather than as a point of reference.

    In doing so, we choose to believe the Damager's stories of *not being ...enough*, and thus look to the outside, to the authority, rather than within.

    When confusion, stress, frustration or hopelessness fill our minds, relying on others for advice seems to make sense. And if those others have reached positions in life we perceive as desirable or authoritative, that convinces us even further.

    But when we look to the outside, we place two sizable obstacles in our path to the mastering the Self.

J. Krishnamurti elegantly stated the first: *"The primary cause of disorder in ourselves is the seeking of reality promised by another."*

The second obstacle is a bit more subtle: the Self is not lost in the first place, and therefore it will not be found through seeking. *The Self is and has always been within us.* **It has only been hidden by our unskillful use of the mind.**

Imagine holding a glass of water while walking around asking where to find water. That makes no sense since you are holding that which you are looking for.

The same applies to mastering the Self. It is not about creating and then mastering an improved self, but rather recognizing what is already within.

We can sidestep this obstacle of looking 'out there' for what we want by trusting our instincts. This will over time and in small steps builds a foundation on which mastery will take hold.

As Carl Jung said: *"who looks outside, dreams; who looks inside, awakens."*

5. **Intellectual Pursuit**. The fifth misunderstanding occurs when we assume that the intellect alone can provide the path to Self-mastery.

    For example: someone makes an intellectual decision to lose weight, or quit smoking. Even though that decision might make logical sense, backed by significant health research, follow-through is often short-lived.

Why is this?

Because the small mind and its four characters can easily distort the intellect, and in turn defeat our intentions. The Reacter comes onto the scene in response to the Ruler having failed in reinforcing how we, others and conditions *should or shouldn't* be. The Damager starts spinning stories about our not being …enough, which will engage the Fixer, who creates the pressure to "repair" ourselves as quickly as possible.

In response, we often act to add yet more to our intellects through books, teachers, workshops and motivational methods. In doing so, *we mistake adding information, and analyzing it, for having achieved actual progress.*

When we make choices based on clear thoughts and emotions, without engaging the negative mind-characters, we have a much greater chance of succeeding in anything we attempt.

We can sidestep the obstacle of 'intellectual pursuit' by learning what it objectively takes to go from points A to B, and asking ourselves how we *feel* about making a firm commitment to do what it takes from start to finish. Follow-through is key.

Respecting how we feel is essential to our success because emotions determine our behaviors and our results.

6. **Comfort Zones**. The sixth misunderstanding occurs when we mistake remaining in our comfort zones for having mastered the Self.

We are instinctually comfort-seeking creatures, and don't care much for uncertainty and risk. This is why our brains will fight anything risky or new.

We like familiarity and predictability, which is why we create habits and comfort zones to minimize risk and stress. For example, we keep our socks in one drawer and underwear in another, which allows us to find them easily every time.

Even though we intellectually know that personal development takes place only when we step outside of our comfort zones, we often struggle to do so, and revert to our old ways fairly quickly in favor of the familiar – *until the next "crisis" shakes us up, and makes us rethink our lives.*

At which point we attempt again, but soon the allurements of safety and familiarity, backed by our risk-averse brains, pulls us back. Every successive attempt creates more resistance, which drains the resiliency we need for following through.

We can sidestep this obstacle of 'limiting ourselves to our comfort zones' by making small changes in things we routinely do.

If you go to lunch at a certain time every day, go ten minutes earlier or later. If you get your coffee from certain place, try a different place once in a while. If you watch TV every night as a way of relaxing, listen to some music instead. If you eat fast, eat slower. If you tell yourself depressing stories which make your mind unproductive, *tell no stories.*

Notice what you do out of habit, then do it differently for a while. Keep breaking your ingrained habits consistently. The mental flexibility you gain will serve you well in your Self-mastery process.

Start small, since big efforts tend to create disappointment. *"We should be able to have our goals in our pocket,"* Gurdjieff used to say. This means they should be small enough so we can achieve them and build a trail of success.

7. **Know Myself**. The seventh misunderstanding occurs when we assume that we must thoroughly "know" our self, and if we don't, we should place it on top of our agendas if we hope to accomplish anything worthwhile.

    This wrongly assumes that there *is* a solid "self" somewhere, which if we dig for we will find, and then able to control.

    However, striving to get to know a self that is constantly changing is like trying to capture the wind, which by its very nature constantly moves and changes.

    Why so? Because we are in an endless state of flux, as every cell in our bodies is constantly changing and being replaced with a new one every seven years on average, according to research by Stanford University. [112]

    The brain, also a collection of cells, changes as we learn and experience new things and interact with others. This, as you'll recall, is neuroplasticity.

So there is really nothing solid about us mentally or physically.

But we create an illusion of "solidness" about the self when we cling to our thoughts, stories and habits. This keeps us within our comfort zones and blocks our progress.

As Harvard psychologist Dan Gilbert eloquently stated: "*Human beings are works in progress that mistakenly think they're finished."*

We often look at ourselves as being "finished" mechanical systems with certain fixed qualities who must work perfectly all the time. If not, we are broken and need fixing.

Just as when we buy a toaster, we expect it to work flawlessly. We certainly do not pay for a "work in progress" toaster.

We habitually extend the same logic to others and conditions by expecting them also work perfectly all the time, and if they don't, they *should* be *fixed* immediately. This fixing, we *falsely believe,* will return everything to perfection.

This idea of being perfect and striving for perfection in ourselves, others and conditions, is a potent source of judgments we levy. In the process, we generate useless thoughts, tension and disconnection.

We can sidestep the obstacle of 'must know myself first' by reminding ourselves that we are *works in progress;* that the *road to Self-mastery is ongoing.*

8. **Magical thinking**. The eighth misunderstanding occurs in thinking that the future will *somehow magically* change in our favor without *conscious effort and practical action.*

   This idea confuses the mind in two principal ways.

   First in thinking that an *unknown future* somehow *knows* what is good for us. This energizes illusory thinking – a habit of the small mind.

   Second, making meaningful change becomes harder as we grow older, thus by embracing that illusion we further delay taking productive actions.

We can sidestep the obstacle of 'magical thinking,' on waiting on an illusory future, by becoming proactive and promptly put to use what we learn.

As Winston Churchill put it: *"success is not final, failure is not fatal: it is the courage to continue that counts."*

9. **Artificial Positivism**. The ninth misunderstanding occurs when we confuse artificial positivism for having mastered the Self.

   When we attempt to be 'positive' by ignoring and rejecting the "unpleasant" or looking the other way, we are in fact trying to undo the brain's natural Negativity Bias. This cannot be done.

   In the process, we prevent ourselves from correctly seeing and dealing with objective reality.

It is in our ability to productively direct our thoughts, *not* in pointlessly manipulating ourselves that we advance toward Self-mastery.

The Greek philosopher Epictetus expresses it precisely: *"It's not what happens to you, but how you react to it that matters."*

In other words, it's not the brain's negativity that makes the difference, it is how we view it and deal with it.

We can sidestep the obstacle of trying to be 'artificially positive' by remembering this aspect of how our brains work, and that it will remain unchangeable.

10. **Big Bang**. The tenth misunderstanding is when we expect to master the Self in a single instant, a big bang, marking the end of our journey.

    We will set ourselves up for major disappointment by embracing this illusion.

    Self-mastery is a gradual unfolding process dependent on continuing practice. It is ongoing with no specific termination point. What we know so far, scientifically and otherwise, has revealed no limits to human consciousness.

We can sidestep this obstacle, expecting a 'big bang,' by befriending our Ruler which tells us how we *should be*, the Damager, which spins not good... enough stories, and the Fixer, which demand immediate perfection.

The Self is a state of mind, rather than a destination – an experience which entails an increasing sense of inner peace and freedom that emerges quietly.

11. **Time Limit**. The eleventh misunderstanding occurs when we put a time frame within which we *must* achieve Self-mastery.

    We live in a world where *instant* is considered the norm. But the desire to get *there* as quickly as possible becomes a trap because there is no "there" to get to. This makes the notion of time and speed an interference with our process.

As Confucius said: *"It does not matter how slowly you go so long as you do not stop."*

We can sidestep this obstacle of imposing an artificial 'time frame' by befriending our Fixer, which pushes us to get *there* as quickly as possible.

12. **No More Challenges**. The final misunderstanding occurs when we believe that Self-mastery relieves us of *ever* having to deal with life's challenges again.

    Life is what it is, does what it does, and most importantly, changes second-by-second beyond our control. Therefore what life is and does, as well as its challenges, also change constantly, and beyond our control.

    Zen master Dogen addressed this important fact when he said, *"One must be deeply aware of the impermanence of the world."*

How we perceive what we call 'challenging' or 'distressing' determines how we respond, which in turn impacts our thoughts, emotions, behaviors and results.

We can sidestep this obstacle of 'no more challenges' by recognizing that life is a dynamic process, that everything internal and external will soon change, and that our attachment to wanting things to remain as they were causes our tensions.

When we deeply understand that life means constant change, and that its challenges will change just as quickly, that we are neither stuck nor under attack, we begin *befriending life*. We then begin to adapt and resolve life's inevitable challenges in productive ways.

There is an Easier Way

The obstacles we have explored here are the products of unskillful use of our minds. Or to put it more accurately...

It isn't that we use our minds unskillfully -- we often don't use it at all. It uses us.

Instead of bogging down our minds in complex philosophical ideas or manipulating our thoughts and beliefs to make headway, we can simply use the tools we have learned to befriend the small mind and thus tap into the big mind.

This will far more easily deliver a balanced brain and mind, and in turn automatically harmonize our being, doing and creating.

True personal power and mastery of the Self lie in choosing which thoughts to allow and which thoughts to drop.

An excellent poem by Portia Nelson charmingly describes the process of learning to choose in five steps. It reads as follows:

There's a Hole in My Sidewalk: The Romance of Self Discovery in Five Steps:

1. *I walk down the street.*

   There is a deep hole in the sidewalk. I fall in. I am lost . . . I am hopeless.

   It isn't my fault. It takes forever to find a way out.

2. *I walk down the same street.*

   There is a deep hole in the sidewalk. I pretend I don't see it. I fall in again.

   I can't believe I am in the same place.

   But, it isn't my fault. It takes a long time to get out. I walk down the same street.

   There is a deep hole in the sidewalk. I see it is there. I still fall in . . . it's a habit.

   My eyes are open. I know where I am. It is my fault. I get out immediately.

3. *I walk down the same street. There is a deep hole in the sidewalk. I walk around it.*

4. *I walk down another street.*

It's your choice, with you in charge

Nineteen

How Can I Really?

This book proposes that only we can lead ourselves to where we want to go. But where is that?

How can we *really* master the Self, and as a result overcome fear, dissolve stress, quiet the mind, think productively, feel happier, love, accept and trust ourselves, experience freedom, feel stronger, and produce fulfilling results – which we all envision for our lives?

This book proposes that we can accomplish what we envision for ourselves through a learning process of discovering *who we are beyond our thoughts*, developing new skills, and intentionally leading ourselves toward mastery of our minds.

To aid us in reliably go through this process, we covered modern brain and cognitive sciences, side-by-side with ancient wisdom and teachings, to validate the approach offered.

We explored the brain, the inner working of the mind, and how specific thinking modes – the small mind and it four negative characters – can make our journey to Self-mastery challenging and at times seemingly impossible.

We then discovered how through simple neuroscience-based tools and practices we can sidestep those mind barriers and move ourselves toward mastery and the big mind.

This has been the premise of this book.

You carry the promise of this book within yourself since *only you can lead yourself,* through effort and practice, *to Self-mastery.*

It's that simple; *you don't need anyone else to accomplish it.* You now have the knowledge, the methods and the tools. All you need to get "there" is effort and practice.

My hope, at this point, is that everything you've read so far and everything you've experienced through the practices has led you to this conclusion:

There is nothing wrong with you, at any level, despite what your thoughts and stories may be telling you, and despite what you may have been told by others.

You are not broken or damaged, and require no fixing.

Although I don't know you personally, and don't know anything about your life experiences, I would like to ask you to consider the following, which I believe is applicable to us all:

Our inner core cannot be damaged in anyway or by anyone, regardless of what we have been through in our lives.

Life can bend us out of shape. But we cannot be broken.

Although most of us have had distressing experiences, it is only *our thoughts in the present moment* that re-create those experiences. This is not to discount the influence of past events. However, *the brain does not recognize past or future. It only knows the present.* Anything from the past that appears *real in the present moment does so only because of the brain's activity.*

T.S. Eliot stated it well: *"What is this self inside us, this silent observer, severe and speechless critic, who can terrorize us and urge us on to futile activity and in the end, judge us still more severely for the errors into which his own reproaches drove us?"*

The "self inside us" he refers to is the small mind expressing itself through its four characters that hide in the shadows that we have not yet acknowledged or befriended.

We come to master the Self when we befriend all that we are: the beauty and the beast, all under one skin.

Carl Rogers speaks to this critical idea: *"The curious paradox is that when I accept myself just as I am, then I can change."*

Leading Toward Mastery

To master our Self we *first* need to *realize that we are not our thoughts, good, bad or indifferent.* Thoughts, the product of small drops of chemical transmissions in our brains, are only tools to help us survive and find our ways in the world. *That is all.* There is no need to believe them, especially if they are distorted, which they often are.

Self-mastery begins with the right understanding that who we are is far greater than our thoughts. When we realize that we are not our thoughts, our identities, our accomplishments or lack of them, and our past or our imagined future, we then come to realize that **we are the thinker and not the thought**.

This near immediately frees us from the influence of the small mind.

It is in that clarity that the mind regains its calm natural state, and we experience the Self.

The great Zen teacher D.T. Suzuki called this "returning to one's home." He said, "You have now found yourself. From the very beginning, nothing has been kept away from you. It was yourself that closed the eye to the face. There is nothing to explain, nothing to teach, that will add to you."

The Self is just what it is. It needs no prodding or shaping. It does not depend on positive thinking, accomplishment, intelligence, social stature, problem solving or achieving more or better.

It has no religion, belief, ideology, gender, race, age or nationality.

It is not a destination which goal setting can take us to.

There is nothing to see because to see it one must assume that it is localized in a particular place.

To master the Self using control makes it move farther away.

The Self is an experience that words, thoughts and concepts cannot describe.

The beauty of it is that it appears as soon as we befriend our small mind at which time the mind return to its calm natural state. What we then experience is a state that flows effortlessly because the two minds are working harmoniously together.

There's a poem by Kalu Rinpoche that sums all this up nicely:

"We live in illusion and the appearance of things.
There is a reality, we are that reality.
When you understand this, you will see 'you' are nothing.
And, being nothing, you are everything."

Leading the self toward mastery is neither a philosophical nor esoteric undertaking. Rather, it is a tangible and scientifically describable process at which anyone can succeed using the right tools.

Let's explore what that process is.

The Process of Mastery

Self-mastery is a five step process:

First we must *value* Self-mastery as part of our personal growth and development rather than as a springboard in the pursuit of *more* and *better*.

Second, we must genuinely accept that the Self is not outside of us. Carl Jung called realizing the Self an *"inside job"* -- meaning the Self is not somewhere else; it has always been and will remain within us.

An old story tells of a small fish who hears a tale about the ocean. It sounds like a wonderful place, and he immediately sets out to find it. But swimming far and wide, he cannot find any sign of this thing called "the ocean." Finally, he meets a wise old fish who tells him that he is already swimming in the ocean, and no longer needs to search for it. The little fish is overcome with joy.

We, like the little fish, believe that the ocean – or Self – is somewhere out there, yet we have been swimming in it all along. We are not separate from it, cut off from it, and do not need to look for it. *All we need is to sidestep the obstacles the small mind creates which obstruct our view of it.*

Third, since it *is* an inside job, only we can lead ourselves to our Self. No one can do it for us, regardless of who they are or what they have accomplished; not a teacher, master, minister, leader or friend. Only we can do it, and only though our own conscious and ongoing effort.

That is why I call this process Self-mastery and made *you* the promise of this book.

Fourth, *to seek the Self directly is to deny that one is already the Self.* Searching for it simply makes it fade from our view. Stress and anxiety mask it. **It is of outmost importance that we understand and accept this paradox.**

Have you ever observed a cat trying to catch its own tail? More and harder he tries, farther away the tail moves. Only when he stops trying the tail curls back toward him.

The same applies to us. The best thing we can do is to *master our mind and lead it to its calm natural state where the Self resides.*

We could call it God, Christ, Nirvana, the Tao, Allah, the Buddha nature, the present moment, awareness, pure consciousness or the big mind. The label we attach to it makes no difference.

Yet we know it once we experience it. *That is the natural paradox that resolves itself when we take the indirect path – rather than directly looking for the Self – by removing the barriers that conceal it.*

The indirect path naturally resolves paradoxes, removes barriers and directs us toward the Self.

Fifth, we can only begin the process exactly where we are right now, rather than waiting until we are locked into a monastery, exotic practices, and intellectual pursuit of yet more answers, or become lost in chasing the dream of *more* and *better*.

All five steps together lead us to mastering our Self. And this entire process begins with our intentional self-leadership, scientifically known as self-directed neuroplasticity, or emotional regulation.

What is Self-Leadership?

We have used the terms self-leadership, self-directed neuroplasticity and emotional regulation throughout the book.

Let's see what they are, and how they relate to each other.

What is *emotional regulation?* The word emotion, derived from Latin, means to *move.* Emotions – energy in motion – arise when we perceive a given situation as either relevant or not relevant to our foremost instinctual goal: to feel safe and secure.

Emotions generate behavior by sending chemical signals to the muscles and organs, energizing them and preparing us to act physically.

Emotional regulation, therefore, is the skill of managing our emotions so that our behaviors which follow are appropriate and beneficial.

What is *neuroplasticity?* Neuroplasticity means that the brain is plastic, flexible and changes its neural formation with new learning and experience. For example, if we initially learn that a car is a box that moves, and later add the experience of moving the car by driving it, we effectively change our brain's neural formation and function.

How do emotional regulation and neuroplasticity interact?

We know that emotions are agents that change the brain in real and lasting ways. We've also learned that our emotions follow our thoughts, meaning that the nature of our thoughts determines the quality of our emotions.

Therefore by appropriately regulating our thoughts and therefore our emotions, we change our brain's circuitry for the better.

Where do self-leadership and Self-mastery interact?

Again, we have a three way thought-to-emotion-to-brain cycle. Among the three, our thoughts are the only part we can directly access and manage to productively impact our emotions, and to change our brains for the better.

Self-leadership is therefore the skill to monitor and productively direct our thoughts. This in turn influences our emotions, improves our brains, and we behave more in our long-term interests, consistent with our deepest values.

Self-mastery occurs when we take sole responsibility for leading the self; hence, the role of self-leadership.

How do we develop self-leadership skills? It is a three part process:

1. **Monitoring:** Listening to our thoughts without accepting them as true or acting on them;
2. **Directing:** Deciding which thoughts are worth paying attention to, and
3. **Choosing:** Selecting the productive thoughts.

As you'll recall, these methods are the same steps we use in thought labeling.

Learning to effectively direct one's thoughts is the first core skill in the process of Self-mastery.

Aristotle clarifies the importance of this point in saying: *"It is the mark of an educated mind to be able to entertain a thought without accepting it."*

Self-leadership is a skill which can be learned.

What is Action?

Action is the bridge that allows us to travel the distance between where we are now to where we want to go.

Inaction, or inconsistent action, is often what prevents us from achieving our desired results.

Inaction – waiting for conditions to be perfect, intellectual rationales, procrastination and so on – distracts us *because they are risk free, and we don't like risk*. It is therefore quite tempting.

Effective action on the other hand helps us achieve our intended results. It has three principles:

First, only by our *own* actions can we lead ourselves.

Second, while action is inherently energizing, the initial excitement can fade when we encounter the inevitable challenges inherent to any new undertaking.

Third, when excitement fades, consistent follow-through is the most important step we need to cross the bridge successfully.

Why so? Because only with persistence and resiliency do we avoid giving up, which if we do the mind records as a "failure," making our next endeavor even more challenging.

Doing the exercises and using the tools throughout the book on a consistent basis is the essence of action and follow-through.

William Jams emphasis the importance of action in saying: "*Action may not bring happiness. But there is no happiness without action.*"

The more we practice recognizing and befriending the four negative mind-characters, the more quickly and deeply we return the mind to it calm natural state, and the more productive we will become in all areas of our lives.

The essence of practice is action in the here and now to help ourselves step out of our habitual patterns and comfort zones. We can start by using our daily chores such as taking a shower, eating breakfast, interacting with family, going to work, relating to coworkers, cooking dinner and taking out the trash as opportunities for ongoing practice.

We soon will view all of our experiences as mastery practice. *Every step of the journey is the journey itself.*

Succeeding in our actions requires resilience.

What is Resilience?

Resilience is the energy, strength and vigor required to handle life's inevitable challenges in productive ways. An important aspect of that productivity is remaining healthy and happy.

Being resilient does not mean that we do not experience difficulty, distress or sadness. It means we are able to consider them objectively, bounce back from their potential setbacks, and move forward.

Resiliency is not a trait that we either have or don't; it is a set of skills we develop. Let's explore how to develop resiliency skill.

1. **Directed Attention:** Our most precious resource is *not* time, but *attention*. When we direct and maintain our attention toward a particular task for the duration needed, we accomplish much. Without it, we spend a lot of time

spinning our wheels and accomplishing very little. *The quality of our attention determines the value we derive from our efforts.*

2. **Productive thinking:** We determine the quality of our being, doing and creating through emotions, which in turn follow our thoughts. Useful thoughts enrich our emotions, boost our energy, and inspire our behavior. Useless thoughts do the opposite. *Useful and productive thinking is the key to sustaining our resilience.*

3. **Steering through challenges:** We will, without doubt, encounter hurdles in our process as we intend to transform our useless thinking habits. The small mind, which likes the same old habits, will initially resist our efforts. We need to monitor *what is useful and what is not, and quickly release useless thoughts to maintain the stamina we need to continue.*

Self-leadership, action and resiliency are the paths by which we advance toward Self-mastery. Like our muscles, we can exercise, develop and strengthen them all.

It's really up to you.

Those who cannot change their
Minds cannot change anything.
~ George Bernard Shaw

Twenty

Onward

The idea of leading the self to the Self, of Self-mastery, reminds me of three-way light bulbs. Each turn of the switch releases more power, and in turn the bulb gets brighter. The third turn lights the bulb the brightest.

In our journey, our minds provide the power, our actions turn the switch, and the bulb is the Self. In this case, though, the bulb has no upper limit in how brightly it can shine.

Our Self will get brighter, and easier to experience, as we supply it with more power through productive thoughts, emotions and behaviors.

With practice, each turn of the switch will become less demanding and more enjoyable.

After awhile our brightness will shine naturally and effortlessly, not only to illuminate our own path, but possibly to inspire others.

The source of all this is our thoughts – the cause of our unhappiness or our joy and freedom.

If I were I to describe this book in one phrase it would be: **we are far more than our thoughts.** *All our challenges begin* *when we mistake who we are with our false and distorted thoughts.*

This factual story reminds me of the power we give our thoughts:

In India, elephants are trained to entertain tourists. When they are still small calves, trainers secure one of their ankles by a thin short rope to a wooden peg. The peg defines the axis around which the calf can circle, and length of the rope determines how far he can walk.

As the elephants mature and grow larger, the years of being restrained conditions them to assume they cannot break free from the thin rope, even though their sheer strength would allow them to easily set themselves free. However, their old belief that the rope is still stronger than they are keeps them in bondage, and serving as circus acts, for the remainder of their lives.

Thoughts for many of us are the peg-like axis around which our lives revolve. We automatically limit our being, doing and creating to the length of the imaginary rope we have attached to an imaginary peg.

When we believe our false thoughts, we cannot differentiate ourselves from them. Therefore, *the quality of our life becomes limited to the last thought passing through our minds.*

This is an unsettling way of being and living, constantly disrupted by the reactive mind.

In closing, I would like to offer two considerations as to why the methods and practices in this book offer an effective method for mastering the Self.

First, the scientifically-based methods and tools provide practical ways to wisely intervene and productively shift our thoughts, which are source of our emotions and behaviors and ultimately our life experiences.

Second, removing the mind obstacles to the Self through an indirect approach eliminates resistance, which is the major source of failure in attempting Self-mastery.

Let's consider these two principles more thoroughly.

We can try to change our beliefs, behaviors, character, motivation, communication style, goals, and the like. But if our thoughts remain fixed at their core, previous patterns soon resurface again.

Shifting the source of our emotions and behaviors – our thoughts – is ultimately the most productive effort.

Imagine yourself standing near a stream, thirsty for water. You notice, however, that the water is muddy and undrinkable. You try to filter it in various ways, but before you can drink, the water has become muddy again. The purity and clarity simply doesn't last no matter how many times you filter it. Why? Because unless you first cleanse the water upstream, it will remain muddy further downstream, where you are standing.

Just the same, our thoughts are the source from which everything else flows. Attempting to change our behavior to create different results poses the same challenge – *it is a temporary approach.*

If we truly want real and lasting change, we must first cleanse our minds of useless thoughts. **Doing so is the essence of mastering the Self.**

You have probably heard Einstein's famous quote: "*Insanity is doing the same thing over and over again and expecting different results.*"

But what if we do things differently and end up with the same results?

Leave one job because the boss is intolerable, and end up at another where the new boss is just like the first? End one relationship, and enter a new one, and it turns out the same?

We've changed our doing, but our results remain constant. Why is that?

Because *the underlying structure of anything determines its behavior.* Similarly, the understructure of our behaviors are our thoughts. *Nothing will change unless they do.*

The methods and tools this book offers are designed to put us in charge of directing our thoughts; to help us develop the skills to master the Self.

As we lead ourselves, we will notice the Self becoming brighter, and increasingly so the more we step out of our confining small minds.

Our daily activities are where our reality is. So why not start here and now?

The key to all this is action. As Buddha asked: *"However many holy words you read, however many you speak, what good will they do if you do not act upon them?"*

Thank you for taking the time to read this book. I hope you have found it to be valuable.

In closing, I would like to share this poem with you:

You wander from room to room, hunting for the diamond necklace that is already around your neck.

Remember, the entrance to the sanctuary is inside you. What you seek is seeking you.

The door is wide and open. Don't go back to sleep.

~ Rumi

Twenty One

Living in Self Mastery

You were born with potential
You were born with goodness and trust
You were born with ideals and dreams
You were born with greatness
You were born with wings
You are not meant for crawling, so don't.

You have wings
Learn to use them, and fly.

~ Rumi

Twenty Two

Practice Glossary

Here you will find a glossary of practices and tools spread throughout the book for your easy reference.

1-	How to Tap into the Big Mind	32
2-	The Brain and the Mind: Key Points	44
3-	The Four Negative Mind-Characters	81
4-	Befriending the Reacter	88
5-	Befriending the Ruler	99
6-	Befriending the Damager	104
7-	Befriending the Fixer	111
8-	Putting it All Together: Key Points	123
9-	Resolving the Paradox	128
10-	Thought Labeling Tool	142

The Author

Nasser D. Salehinia is a brain and cognitive sciences researcher, scholar and writer. He has studied Eastern and Western teachings related to mind, behavior, personal growth and leadership, and has been involved in contemplative practices for the past thirty years. He is a certified Neuro-Linguistics Master Practitioner, and has been involved in personal and professional training and development since 1984.

He began his work as a research scholar and training assistant under the guidance of Dr. Stan Grof, the renowned brain researcher, psychiatrist and the founder of SEN. He continued his training under the direction of Dr. Peter Harding, a physician and psychiatrist with expertise in cognitive, Jungian psychology and Gestalt.

In addition, he has been a founder and CEO of number of successful technology and consulting companies. He is the founder and CEO of YouLeadYou™, an organization offering neuroscience-based training and coaching for individuals and organizations.

About Us

I hope you have enjoyed this book and have found the principles and practices of value.

Our Self-Mastery system introduced in this book utilizes over two and half decades of research in neuroscience and neuropsychology, as well as hands-on experience working with people of all ages, backgrounds and in different settings.

YouLeadYou™ offers trainings for individuals, groups and organizations that carry this book's principles to a much greater depth.

During 6 one-hour weekly sessions, either on-site or online, participants will learn new skills they can easily master and readily use to productively direct their minds, achieve real and lasting change, and attain their personal and professional goals.

For more information about our programs, coaching and speaking engagements, contact us at:

YouLeadYou™
Info@youleadyou.net
831.200.3460
http://youleadyou.net

Scientific References

1. http://www.brainfacts.org/brain-basics/neuroanatomy/
2. http://www.scientificamerican.com/article/why-does-the-brain-need-s/
3. http://www.ncbi.nlm.nih.gov/pmc/articles/PMC2872188/
4. https://en.wikipedia.org/wiki/Brain
5. http://www.ncbi.nlm.nih.gov/pmc/articles/PMC2872188/
6. https://en.wikipedia.org/wiki/Brain
7. http://www.scientificamerican.com/article/do-people-only-use-10-percent-of-their-brains/
8. https://en.wikipedia.org/wiki/Ten_percent_of_the_brain_myth
9. *https://www.psychologytoday.com/articles/200306/our-brains-negative-bias*
10. http://www.apa.org/science/about/psa/2011/10/positive-negative.aspx
11. http://www.loni.usc.edu/about_loni/education/brain_trivia.php
12. http://www.scientificamerican.com/article/do-people-only-use-10-percent-of-their-brains/
13. https://en.wikipedia.org/wiki/Ten_percent_of_the_brain_myth
14. http://www.heartmath.org/research/science-of-the-heart/head-heart interactions.html?submenuheader=3
15. Armour J A, Anatomy and function of the intrathoracic neurons regulating the mammalian heart. In: Zucker I H and Gilmore J P, eds. Reflex Control of the Circulation. Boca Raton, FL, CRC Press: 1-3. (1991)
16. McCraty R, Bradley RT, Tomasino D, the Resonant Heart, Shift: At the Frontiers of Consciousness; 5:15-19. (2004)
17. McCraty R, The Energetic Heart: Bioelectromagnetic Communication Within and Between People, Chapter published in: Clinical Applications of Bioelectromagnetic Medicine, edited by Rosch P J and Markov M S. New York: Marcel Dekker: 541-562. (2004)
18. Armour J. A. Cardiac neuronal hierarchy in health and disease, American journal of physiology, regulatory, integrative and comparative physiology. Aug; 287(2):R262-71. (2004)
19. Tiller W, McCraty R, et al, Cardiac coherence; A new non-invasive measure of autonomic system order. Alternative Therapies in Health and Medicine; 2(1): 52-65. (1996)
20. Rollin McCraty, PhD and Mike Atkinson. In: Proceedings of the Annual Meeting of the Pavlovian Society, Tarrytown, NY. (1999)

21. Influence of afferent cardiovascular input on cognitive performance and alpha activity [Abst.]. Rollin McCraty, PhD and Mike Atkinson. In: Proceedings of the Annual Meeting of the Pavlovian Society, Tarrytown, NY. (1999)
22. Rein G, McCraty R and Atkinson M, the Physiological and Psychological Effects of Compassion and Anger, Journal of Advancement in Medicine; 8(2):87-105. (1995)
23. Rollin McCraty, MA, Mike Atkinson, Dana Tomasino, BA and William A. Tiller, PhD. In: Proceedings of the Fifth Appalachian Conference on Neurobehavioral Dynamics: Brain and Values. Mahwah, NJ: Lawrence Erlbaum Associates. (1997)
24. Rollin McCraty, PhD, Mike Atkinson and William A. Tiller, PhD. In: Proceedings of the Tenth International Montreux Congress on Stress, Montreux, Switzerland. (1999)
25. Rollin McCraty, Ph.D. Mike Atkinson, and Dana Tomasino, B.A. modulation of DNA conformation by heart focused intention, Institute of heartmath. (2003)
26. Rollin McCraty, PhD, William A. Tiller, PhD and Mike Atkinson. In: Proceedings of the Brain-Mind Applied Neurophysiology EEG Neurofeedback Meeting. Key West, Florida. (1996)
27. How default is the default mode of brain function? Further evidence from intrinsic BOLD signal fluctuations. Peter Fransson - MR Research Center, Cognitive Neurophysiology, Dep. of Clinical Neuroscience, Karolinska Institute.
28. Zen and the brain: mutually illuminating topics. James Austin. Department of Neurology, University of Colorado Denver School of Medicine, Denver, CO, USA.
29. The Brain's Default Network Anatomy, Function, and Relevance to Disease (Randy L. Buckner, Jessica R. Andrews-Hanna, and Daniel Schachter.
30. Coactivation of the Default Mode Network regions and Working Memory Network regions during task preparation. Koshino H, Minamoto T, Yaoi K, Osaka M, Osaka N.
31. Idle Minds - Nature| - vol 489 | 20 September 2012
32. Bringing Unconscious Choices to Awareness: 'Default Mode', Body Rhythms, and Hypnosis (David Hartman and Diane Zimberoff - Journal of Heart-Centered Therapies, 2011, Vol. 14, No. 2, pp. 3-75)
33. 21. Coactivation of the Default Mode Network regions and Working Memory Network regions during task preparation - Hideya Koshino1, Takehiro Minamoto2, Ken Yaoi3, Mariko Osaka2 & Naoyuki Osaka3 1Dep. of Psychology, California State University, Dep. of Human Sciences, Osaka University, Dep of Psychology, Kyoto University.

34. The effect of worry and rumination on affect states and cognitive activity. Katie A. Mclaughlin, Thomas D. Borkovec, Nicholas J. Sibrave. University of Washington Department of Psychology.
35. http://psychcentral.com/blog/archives/2011/01/20/why-ruminating-is-unhealthy-and-how-to-stop/
36. http://www.hindawi.com/journals/ijhy/2012/453465/
37. Rethinking Rumination (Susan Nolen-Hoeksema, Blair E. Wisco1 and Sonja Lyubomirsky)
38. Depression and Ruminative Thinking (Madeline Vann, Pat F. Bass)
39. The Effects of Rumination on Psychological and Biological Recovery from Stress in Depression (Joelle LeMoult, University of Miami)
40. Task Positive and Default Mode Networks during a Parametric Working Memory Task in Obstructive Sleep Apnea Patients and Healthy Controls. Olga Prilipko, MD1; Nelly Huynh, PhD1; Sophie Schwartz, PhD2; Visasiri Tantrakul, MD1; Jee Hyun Kim, MD1; Ana Rita Peralta, MD1; Clete Kushida, MD, PhD1; Teresa Paiva, MD, PhD3; Christian Guilleminault, MD. - Stanford University Sleep Clinic and Center for Human Sleep Research, Redwood City, CA; 2Geneva University Medical Center, Geneva, Switzerland; 3Department of Neurology, CENC, Lisbon, Portugal.
41. How default is the default mode of brain function? Further evidence from intrinsic BOLD signal fluctuations. Peter Fransson - MR Research Center, Cognitive Neurophysiology, Dep.of Clinical Neuroscience, Karolinska Institute.
42. Zen and the brain: mutually illuminating topics. James Austin. Department of Neurology, University of Colorado Denver School of Medicine, Denver, CO, USA
43. Buckner, R. L., Andrews-Hanna, J. R., & Schacter, D. L. (2008). The brain's default network. *Annals of the New York Academy of Sciences*, *1124*(1), 1-38.
44. Guo, W., Liu, F., Zhang, J., Zhang, Z., Yu, L., Liu, J. & Xiao, C. (2014). Abnormal Default-Mode Network Homogeneity in First-Episode, Drug-Naive Major Depressive Disorder.
45. Meditation experience is associated with differences in default mode network activity and connectivity. Judson A. Brewer, Patrick D. Worhunsky, Jeremy R. Gray, Yi-Yuan Tang, Jochen Weber, and Hedy Kober Psychological and Cognitive Sciences, 2011 Dec 13; 108(50): 20254–20259
46. Minding the gaps- Go ahead and let your thoughts wander: An 'idle' brain may be the self's workshop. Melissa Healy August 30, 2010
47. Executive Function Fact Sheet By: National Center for Learning Disabilities (NCLD)-(2005)
48. Self-Regulation and the Executive Function: The Self as Controlling Agent. Roy F. Baumeister, Florida State University, Brandon J.

Schmeichel Texas A&M University and Kathleen D. Vohs University of Minnesota.
49. Understanding Executive Functioning Issues – Amanda Morin 20011
50. Executive Functions: A General Overview Copyright 2011 George McCloskey, Ph.D.Philadelphia College of Osteopathic Medicine.
51. The Opposing Domains of Leadership: Integrating Task and Relationship. Kylie Rochford- Department of Organizational Behavior. Weatherhead School of Management. Case Western Reserve University.Cleveland OH.
52. Inside the Mindful Mind: How Mindfulness Enhances Emotion Regulation Through Improvements in Executive Control. Rimma Teper, Zindel V. Segal, and Michael Inzlicht. University of Toronto.
53. The Important Role of Executive Functioning and Self-Regulation in ADHD - Russell A. Barkley, Ph.D.
54. Ego Depletion and Self-Control Failure:An Energy Model of the Self's Executive Function. Roy F. Baumeister, Case Western Reserve University, Cleveland, Ohio, USA
55. Directed Attention as a Common Resource for Executive Functioning and Self-Regulation. Stephen Kaplan1 and Marc G. Berman. Department of Psychology, University of Michigan, Ann Arbor.
56. The Executive Functions and Self-Regulation: An Evolutionary Neuropsychological Perspective, Russell A. Barkley, Ph.D.
57. Unraveling the Knot of Suffering: Combining – neurobiological and Hermeneutic approaches, Hillel D. Braude.
58. Self-Regulation in the Interpersonal Sphere, Kathleen D. Vohs, University of Minnesota, Jannine D. Lasaleta, University of Minnesota, Bob Fennis.
59. Inside the Mindful Mind: How Mindfulness Enhances Emotion Regulation Through Improvements in Executive Control Rimma Teper, Zindel V. Segal, and Michael Inzlicht 1 University of Toronto.
60. Logan GD. Executive control of thought and action. Acta Psychologica.1985
61. http://en.wikipedia.org/wiki/Homeostasis
62. http://biology.about.com/od/biologydictionary/g/homeostasis.htm
63. http://www.neuroanatomy.wisc.edu/coursebook/thalamus.pdf
64. Thalamic relays and cortical functioning S. Murray Sherman. Department of Neurobiology, Pharmacology & Physiology, Univ. of Chicago, Chicago, IL.
65. http://neuroscience.uth.tmc.edu/s4/chapter06.html
66. http://biology.about.com/od/anatomy/p/Amygdala.htm
67. The amygdala and emotion. Gallagher M, Chiba AA.
68. http://thebrain.mcgill.ca/flash/d/d_04/d_04_cr/d_04_cr_peu/d_04_cr_peu.html
69. http://www.caam.rice.edu/~cox/wrap/hippocampus.pdf
70. http://www.icn.ucl.ac.uk/nburgess/papers/Kingetal04.pdf

71. Spatial Memory and Hippocampal Function: Where are we now? Mark Good* Cardiff University
72. http://www.endocrineweb.com/endocrinology/overview-hypothalamus
73. http://courses.cvcc.vccs.edu/wisemand/functions_of_the_hypothalamus.htm
74. http://www.yourhormones.info/glands/hypothalamus.aspx
75. The 10 most important things known about addiction. Doug Sellman, Professor of Psychiatry and Addiction Medicine, National Addiction Centre (NAC), Christchurch, New Zealand.
76. American Psychological Association, "Stress In America (TM): Our Health at Risk" (2012)
77. http://www.loni.usc.edu/about_loni/education/brain_trivia.php
78. American Psychological Association, "Stress In America (TM): Our Health at Risk" (2012)
79. American Institute of Stress, "Stress is Killing You" http://www.stress.org/stress-is-killing-you/
80. Harvard Medical School's Mind-Body Institute. http://www.bensonhenryinstitute.org/index.php/our-research/published-research
81. The Institute of HeartMath "Local and Nonlocal Effects of Coherent Heart Frequencies on Conformational Changes of DNA.
82. P. Kinderman et al, "Psychological Processes Mediate the Impact of Familial Risk, Social circumstances and Life Events on Mental Health", PLOS (2013).
83. N. D. Powell et al "Social stress up-regulates inflammatory gene expression in the leukocyte transcriptome via- adrenergic induction of myelopoiesis". PNAS (2013);
84. S. Cohen at al "Psychological Stress and Disease" Journal of the American Medical Association (2007)
85. S. Cohen et al, "Chronic stress, glucocorticoid receptor resistance, inflammation, and disease risk", PNAS (2012)
86. W. C. Willett, "Balancing Lifestyle and Genomics Research for Disease Prevention," Science 296 (2002): 695– 98
87. C. B. Pert, Molecules of Emotion: Why You Feel the Way You Feel (New York: Simon and Schuster, 1997)
88. Bruce. Lipton, The Biology of Belief: Unleashing the Power of Consciousness, Matter and Miracles (Santa Cruz, CA: Mountain of Love Productions, 2008)
89. Dr. Brian Luke Seaward- http://www.brianlukeseaward.com/downloads/SuperStress-WELCOA-Seaward.pdf
90. www.stress.org
91. Cancer Statistics and Views of Causes Science News Vol.115, No 2. Jan.13 1979, p.23

92. W.C Willett- balancing lifestyle and genomics research for disease prevention Science (296) p 695-698, 2002."Conflict and Your Brain aka "The Amygdala Hijacking"
93. Freedman, Joshua. "Hijacking of the Amygdala"
94. The Relationship between Workplace Stressors and Mortality and Health Costs in the United States.
95. Nature June 1, 2015
96. The Silver Ink June 7, 2015
97. Medicine Net June 5, 2015
98. Finkenauer, Catrin; Vohs, Kathleen D. (2001). "Bad is stronger than good" (PDF). Review of General Psychology 5 (4): 323–370.
99. http://en.wikipedia.org/wiki/Attention
100. Begg, I.M., Anas, A., & Farinacci, S. (1992). Dissociation of processes in belief: source recollection, statement familiarity, and the illusion of truth. Journal of Experimental Psychology, 121, 446-458.
101. Jacoby & Witherspoon, L.L & D. (1982). "Remembering without awareness." Canadian Journal of Psychology/Revue canadienne de psychologie 36 (2): 300. doi:10.1037/h0080638
102. Hasher, Goldstein, and Toppino (1977)
103. Hamilton, Marryellen. "Measuring Implicit Memory". youtube.com. St. Peter's College. Retrieved 2012-04-21.
104. Harlene Rovee-Collier, Hayne (2001). The Development of Implicit and Explicit Memory. John Benjamins Publishing Company. Retrieved 2012-04-18.
105. Putting Feelings Into Words: Affect Labeling Disrupts Amygdala Activity in Response to Affective Stimuli. Matthew D. Lieberman, Naomi I. Eisenberger, Molly J. Crockett, Sabrina M. Tom, Jennifer H. Pfeifer, and Baldwin M. Way. *Psychological Science* 2007;18(5)
106. Subjective Responses to Emotional Stimuli During Labeling, Reappraisal, and Distraction. Matthew D. Lieberman, Tristen K. Inagaki, Golnaz Tabibnia, and Molly Crockett. *Emotion* 2011;11(3)
107. Neural Mechanisms of Symptom Improvements in Generalized Anxiety Disorder Following Mindfulness Training. Britta K. Hölzel, Elizabeth A. Hoge, Douglas N. Greve, Tim Gard, J. David Creswell, Kirk Warren Brown, Lisa Feldman Barrett, Carl Schwartz, Dieter Vaitl, Sara W. Lazar. *NeuroImage: Clinical* 2013;2:448-458
108. Freud, S. (1920). *Beyond the pleasure principle*. SE, 18: 1-64.
109. Freud, S. (1923). *The ego and the id*. SE, 19: 1-66.
110. Carducci, B. (2009). *The psychology of personality: Viewpoints.*
111. Engler, B. (2009). *Personality theories*. Boston: Houghton Mifflin Harcourt Publishing.
112. http://stemcell.stanford.edu/research/

General References

- Austin James H.
  - Zen and the Brain: Toward an Understanding of Meditation and Consciousness
  - Zen-Brain Horizons: Toward a Living Zen
  - Meditating Selflessly: Practical Neural Zen
- Barrett Frank
  - Appreciative Inquiry: A Positive Approach to Building cooperative Capacity
- Beck Charlotte J.
  - Everyday Zen
  - Nothing Special
  - Living Everyday Zen
  - Ordinary Mind: Exploring the Common Ground of Zen and Psychoanalysis
- Block Stanley H. and Block Carolyn B.
  - Mind-Body Workbook for PTSD
- Boorstein Sylvia
  - It's Easier Than You Think: The Buddhist Way to Happiness
  - Don't Just Do Something, Sit There
  - Pay Attention, for Goodness' Sake: The Buddhist Path of Kindness
  - Happiness Is an Inside Job: Practicing for a Joyful Life
- Brown Brene
  - The Gifts of Imperfection: Let Go of Who You Think You're Supposed to Be and Embrace Who You Are
  - Daring Greatly: How the Courage to Be Vulnerable Transforms the Way We Live, Love, Parent, and Lead
- Campbell Joseph
  - The Hero with a Thousand Faces
  - The Power of Myth
  - The Hero's Journey

- Csikszentmihalyi Mihaly
  - Flow
  - Finding Flow: The Psychology Of Engagement With Everyday Life.
- Chodron Pema
  - When Things Fall Apart: Heart Advice for Difficult Times
  - The Places That Scare You: A Guide to Fearlessness in Difficult Times
  - Taking the Leap: Freeing Ourselves from Old Habits and Fears
  - Start Where You Are: A Guide to Compassionate Living
  - Comfortable with Uncertainty: 108 Teachings on Cultivating Fearlessness and Compassion
  - The Wisdom of No Escape: And the Path of Loving-Kindness
- Cooperider, David and Diana Whitney
  - Appreciative Inquiry: A positive Resolution in Change
  - The Appreciative Inquiry Hand Book For Leaders of Change
- Erickson Milton H.
  - Conversations With Milton H. Erickson, M.D.: Changing Individuals
  - Healing in Hypnosis
  - Hypnotic Realities: The Induction of Clinical Hypnosis and Forms of Indirect Suggestion
  - The February Man: Evolving Consciousness and Identity in Hypnotherapy
  - The Nature of Hypnosis and Suggestion
  - Hypnotic Alteration of Sensory Perceptual and Psychophysical Processes
  - Creative Choice in Hypnosis
  - Experiencing Hypnosis: Therapeutic Approaches to Altered States
  - Phoenix: Therapeutic Patterns of Milton H. Erickson
  - My Voice Will Go with You: The Teaching Tales of Milton H. Erickson
  - Patterns of the Hypnotic Techniques of Milton H. Erickson, M.D. Volume 1
  - Uncommon Therapy: The Psychiatric Techniques of Milton H. Erickson, M.D.
- Grinder John and Bandler Richard
  - Origins of Neuro Linguistic Programming
  - Frogs into Princes

- Reframing Neuro Linguistic Programming
- The NLP Field Guide
- Trance Formation
- The Structure of Magic
- Turtles All the Way Down

- Hammond Sue
  - The Think Book of Appreciative Inquiry
- Hanh Thich Nhat
  - Peace Is Every Step: The Path of Mindfulness in Everyday Life
  - The Heart of the Buddha's Teaching: Transforming Suffering into Peace, Joy, and Liberation
  - No Death, No Fear
  - Fear: Essential Wisdom for Getting Through the Storm
  - You Are Here: Discovering the Magic of the Present Moment
  - Silence: The Power of Quiet in a World Full of Noise
  - Reconciliation: Healing the Inner Child
  - Being Peace
- Huber Cheri
  - There Is Nothing Wrong with You: Going Beyond Self-Hate
  - I Don't Want To, I Don't Feel Like It: How Resistance Controls Your Life and What to Do About It
  - Be the Person You Want to Find: Relationship and Self-Discovery
  - What You Practice Is What You Have: A Guide to Having the Life You Want
  - Making a Change for Good: A Guide to Compassionate Self-Discipline
  - Transform Your Life: A Year of Awareness Practice
  - The Depression Book: Depression as an Opportunity for Spiritual Growth
  - The Fear Book: Facing Fear Once and for All
  - The Key: And the Name of the Key Is Willingness
  - How to Get from Where You Are to Where You Want to Be
  - That Which You Are Seeking Is Causing You to Seek
  - When You're Falling, Dive: Acceptance, Freedom and Possibility
  - Suffering Is Optional: Three Keys to Freedom and Joy
  - There Is Nothing Wrong With You: Regardless of What You Were Taught to Believe

- Nothing Happens Next: Responses to Questions About Meditation
- Unconditional Self-Acceptance: The Do-It-Yourself Course
- How You Do Anything Is How You Do Everything: A Workbook

- Satir Virginia
  - People Making
  - Your Many Faces
  - The Satir Model: The Family Model and Beyond
  - Self-Esteem
  - Conjoint Family Therapy

- Siegel Daniel J.
  - Mindsight: The New Science of Personal Transformation
  - Pocket Guide to Interpersonal Neurobiology: An Integrative Handbook of the Mind
  - The Mindful Brain: Reflection and Attunement in the Cultivation of Well-Being

- Stone Hal, Stone Sidra
  - Embracing Ourselves: The Voice Dialogue Manual
  - Embracing Your Inner Critic: Turning Self-Criticism into a Creative Asset
  - Partnering: A new kind of Relationship

- Suzuki D.T.
  - An Introduction to Zen Buddhism
  - The Zen Doctrine of No Mind
  - Zen Buddhism: Selected Writings
  - Manual of Zen Buddhism

- The Dalai Lama
  - The Universe in a Single Atom: The Convergence of Science and Spirituality
  - The Art of Happiness, 10th Anniversary Edition: A Handbook for Living
  - How to See Yourself As You Really Are
  - Healing Anger: The Power Of Patience From A Buddhist Perspective
  - The Meaning of Life: Buddhist Perspectives on Cause and Effect

- Tolle Eckhart
  - The Power of Now: A Guide to Spiritual Enlightenment

- Watts Alan
  - The Wisdom of Insecurity
  - The Book: On the Taboo Against Knowing Who You Are
  - The Way of Zen
  - Become What You Are
  - Tao: The Watercourse Way
  - Still the Mind
  - Does It Matter?: Essays on Man's Relation to Materiality
  - Do You Do It or Does It Do You?: How to Let the Universe Meditate You
  - Nature, Man and Woman
  - The Supreme Identity
  - What Is Tao?
  - Psychotherapy East and West
  - The Meaning of Happiness: The Quest for Freedom of the Spirit in Modern Psychology and the Wisdom of the East
- Whitney Diana and Troston-Bloom Amanda
  - The Power of Appreciative Inquiry: A Practical Guide to Positive Change

Made in the USA
San Bernardino, CA
13 January 2017